The ABC's of Woodworking for Smart Kids

Mind-blowing DIY Project Ideas to become a Little Master in Carving and Woodworking. A Beginners Guide to Learn and Improve your Skills and Techniques.

Micheal Grey

© **Copyright 2024 Micheal Grey - All rights reserved.**

The content contained within this book may not be reproduced, duplicated or transmitted without direct written permission from the author or the publisher.

Under no circumstances will any blame or legal responsibility be held against the publisher, or author, for any damages, reparation, or monetary loss due to the information contained within this book. Either directly or indirectly.

Legal Notice:

This book is copyright protected. This book is only for personal use. You cannot amend, distribute, sell, use, quote or paraphrase any part, or the content within this book, without the consent of the author or publisher.

Disclaimer Notice:

Please note the information contained within this document is for educational and entertainment purposes only. All effort has been executed to present accurate, up to date, and reliable, complete information. No warranties of any kind are declared or implied. Readers acknowledge that the author is not engaging in the rendering of legal, financial, medical or professional advice. The content within this book has been derived from various sources. Please consult a licensed professional before attempting any techniques outlined in this book.

By reading this document, the reader agrees that under no circumstances is the author responsible for any losses, direct or indirect, which are incurred as a result of the use of information contained within this document, including, but not limited to, errors, omissions, or inaccuracies.

Table of Contents

Introduction... 6

Chapter 1...15
Woodworking Skills and Benefits for Kids

Chapter 2 22
Development Stages

Chapter 3 28
Equipment and Tools

Chapter 4 55
How to familiarize tools to kids`

Chapter 5 56
How to Use Tools

Chapter 6 61
Safety System

Chapter 7..**65**

The Techniques

- Hammering
- Sawing
- Drilling

Chapter 8 .... **81**

Measurement

Chapter 9 ....**86**

DIY Woodworking Projects

- Bird Houses
- Toothbrush Holders
- Banana Holder
- Lego Coat Hanger
- Wooden Box Planter
- X-Shaped Minimal Coaster Set
- DIY Children's Wooden Texture Stamps
- Children's First Tool Kit Box
- Tree DIY Swing
- Folding Dollhouse

- Family Name from a Pallet
- Simple Homemade Candy Dispenser
- Simple Hinged Box
- Easy Projects for Smaller Kids

Conclusion 150

Introduction

In the early years of the 1980s and 1990s in the United Kingdom, woodworking was then pretty much eliminated. This occurred due to strict health and safety measures and a concurrent shift in educational preferences; this has occurred.

In more recent times, there has been a renewed worldwide interest in woodwork. This interest occurred alongside the rise of Forest Schools, the schools' tweaking movement, and creating spaces.

The Sloyd woodworking education system, introduced during the last part of the 19th century in the United States, was designed to be an aspect of general education. Sloyd viewed woodworking as an essential developmental resource for all children, unlike vocational programs designed to introduce students to jobs in the market.

The belief seemed to be that brain development was supported and encouraged by the hands' usage, advanced the intellect and trust in countless ways, and developed higher respect for labor compassion. Those feelings are true for anyone who's ever done carpentry or taught woodwork.

In the Wood Working System of Sloyd, the Superintendent of

Schools in New York City, cited the opinion of an unidentified writer.

As the growth of the motor is focused in the brain depends to a great extent on youths movements and exercises, it will be easily understood how vital the nature of the role played by the initial exercise of the hand is.

There is no doubt that in the growth of these motor centers, the most active era is from the fourth to the fourteenth year, after which they become relatively static and stubborn.

Therefore, it can be understood that boys and girls whose hands have been left completely untrained until the fourteenth year are subsequently virtually incapable of greater manual efficiency.

Basically, use it and evolve it early; otherwise, you'll never have it. If kids were not given a chance to explore and evolve the use of one's hands, they would be robbed of their maximum use of them as adults. During the time of intense industrial growth in the US, when the industrial sector's success was based on the productivity and manual dexterity of workers, this was a major concern. But Sloyd went even further in his belief that the use of the hands influenced the brain's development, not just the other way round. Modern research has widely confirmed this belief. Biomechanical modifications in the hand allowed a significantly wider range of hand and finger grips and movements; for more complicated and developed hand movements, the brain created ample control mechanisms.

These changes took place over millions of years, and it is appropriate to say that the brain human and hand co-evolved as a behavior system due to the mutual interdependence of hand and brain. This same hand-brain partnering exists evolutionarily for every living human being as a developmental guidance system.

Every oven of us, starting at birth, is conditioned primarily through the

organization of our hands to start engaging our world and develop our intelligence.

The source of our wisdom and the essence of our humanity is the utilization of our hands that try to influence our presence's materials into entities of beauty and purpose.

Education that does not engage our children's hands in creating and shaping objects does not activate the procedures by which intellect is delivered. Instead of the diverse three-dimensional graphic and thematic tapestry of physical experience, it provides a flat-screened two-dimensional wilderness of lost possibility and failed engagement.

We initiated our woodworking system in high school. We gradually expanded projects into the lower grades, inspired by Sloyd. As we became more aware of the important role of the hands in developing basic human intellect, Our first woodworking projects in elementary school were projects

proposed by teachers in different grades in the classroom. Still, out of significance in Sloyd, we began to do tasks drawn almost directly from initial teacher training handbooks in Sloyd, designed to fully express Sloyd's philosophy. What an efficient place to start than at the outset. For most woodworkers, a pencil sharpener that is hardly anything more than a bit of wood with coarse sandpaper attached

on may seem extremely simple, but must be comprehended in the light of Sloyd's ideology, which suggests that training should move progressively: from the identified to the undiscovered; from the easy to the harder; from the simplistic to the more complicated; from the concrete to the esoteric.

Furthermore, Sloyd's philosophy asks that projects be helpful and appropriate to kids and their families' lives. The simplistic pencil sharpener design creates a starting point in the usages of various woodworking instruments, creating an object beneficial to the student in their other schoolwork, an item still productive in the hands of expert craftsmen and designers. It is not entirely reliant on absolute success precision. If measuring is not accurate, or if sawing is not completely symmetrical, the child's work product will still be a helpful object. In the use of tools, there is no need for attention to detail. In time, this may come. Pencil sharpeners give the production much more pleasure than I've ever dreamed possible. And who knows that making a pencil sharper with basic tools could be the main step in your child's pleasure to work with wood.

By reinforcing children's character through woodworking, our sole objective is to promote self-reliance, cultivate concentration, coach dedication, promote neatness, and instill gratitude for labor, all of which will equip them for their future.

Woodworking Experience seeks to use "working with one's hands" as a natural and human activity to establish the educational thoroughness of children's minds and bodies and solve existing gaps in our academic system. Sloyd is much more than child carpentry - the guiding message behind Sloyd is central. The full ten lists of

SLOYD education objectives are impressive:

- To inculcate a taste for work in general and an appreciation for it.
- Building compassion for hard, sincere, physical work.
- Independence and self-reliance to evolve.
- To provide the habits of order, precision, neatness, and tidiness
- with training.
- To instruct the eye to see precisely and to admire the sense of
- form in beauty.
- To create the feeling of touch and give the hands general
- dexterity.
- To instill focus, industry, dedication, and patience.
- To foster the development of the physical powers of the body.
- Acquiring skill in the use of instruments.

- To perform precise work and to generate useful goods.

We have tried to incorporate sloyd's objectives in this book and aim to teach children the following:

Children must undergo a certain degree of liberty and risk in terms of developing self-reliance and trust. We must grant the 'dignity of risk' to our children; if we constantly strip their risk, we constantly strip their dignity away.

We have an ambition of modifying the overprotection methods that are stealing possibilities during their developmental years to experience risk, commitment, and loss away from children. We focus on creating self-reliant kids who are resistant and able to cope when challenged with real problems.

It is a phenomenal and notable fact, derived from observation, that not only have children in Sloyd work become attentive, but they have also converted this power of participation to other subjects.

We aim to teach children how to resolve their difficulties with focus and memory through purposeful instruction and mentoring.

Besides, we can reduce our societal addiction to relaxation and immediate gratification. Instead, we can instill the importance of delayed fulfillment - equipping kids with the perseverance and grit needed to perform long, challenging tasks.

There is no doubt at all that the habits of order, accuracy, cleanliness, and neatness have an unquestionable value in common life, and therefore we should aim to grow them.

Despite the ban on society, which viewpoint must first be overcome, the bias against manual work is overcome; children love it. We need to stimulate and not suppress children's activity and set it enjoyably along the channel that will lead to work habits.

By fostering our youth, a love and respect for labor, we have the ambition to bridge the difference between the cultural classes in the United States. We believe that children exposed to a suitable degree of manual work will lead to stronger respect and compassion for all social classes, regardless of the career path the children continue to pursue.

Sloyd is not concerned with meeting the needs of the economy or the workforce. It is about trying to respond to a child's inherent needs.

Chapter 1
Woodworking Skills and Benefits for Kids

In early childhood schooling, the importance of woodworking is building confidence and offering a foundation for future learning. "As children create with wood, they learn skills to shape their world."

The concept of young children operating with real tools surprises many, but woodwork has a longstanding history in early education that goes back to Froebel's Kindergarten days. It has nearly disappeared in recent decades, but it is now making a return with growing interest from around the world. There is a noisy revolution taking place!

There is a truly special thing about woodwork. It is so distinct from other operational activities. The scent and feel of wood, the use of real instruments, the use of natural materials, the hammering and sawing sounds, the hands and minds are operating together to interpret their imagination and solve problems, the use of power and coordination: all combined to grab the interest of young children. It offers a truly distinctive experience.

What about safety?! As long as certain basic safety measures are adopted, and appropriate tools are being used, woodwork is a lowrisk activity.

Children's behavior on the woodwork bench is

exemplary; they are involved and do something they enjoy. It is also essential for kids to experience risks and challenges in a controlled environment to learn how to make judgments and decisions to safeguard themselves. This experience is an essential part of child development.

Mind's Creative and Critical Development

Today, woodwork teachers regularly observe outstanding engagement levels, with deep focus and concentration accompanied by persistence and perseverance with challenging tasks, particularly with complicated problem song lv. Woodwork is an amazing medium for communicative art and creative development. It also has the advantage of providing a truly cross-curricular activity to encompass many other learning and development requirements.

Computational thinking is created, scientific knowledge is acquired, technological understanding is created by working with tools, and as they build, children become engineers. As children interact and experiment with wood and instruments' options and go on to convey opinions and resolve their work, woodwork is outstanding for improving children's critical and creative thinking abilities. But woodwork is not just about what kids do; it's about the changes taking place within the child. Woodworking has a considerable impact on children's self-esteem and trust and creates a sense of organization, that can-do" mindset. Woodwork is a platform for kids to express their imagination and creativity. It is relevant not to establish projects whereby all children create the same object. The key to children staying really involved in woodwork is that they are pursuing their own desires and solving their own issues to create their job. When it is initiated and guided by children, all experimentation becomes much more meaningful.

They will set the groundwork to become the inventive innovators of the future by developing their critical and creative thinking capabilities.

Initially, their job is often strictly experimental, tinkering with the materials and instruments' possibilities. In a variety of creative ways, children then go on to express their imagination by creating stuff that they find personally interesting. They tend to lean from literal work to conceptual and more abstract work to more complex constructions.

Practical Skills and Education

In the woodwork process, design and practical skills are combined. Design requires identifying the task, attempting to make a plan of action, evaluating how to proceed, and optimizing and reacting appropriately as the work evolves. The technical skills or craft evolve the designs into stuff. As work is often flexible and evolving as kids adapt, refine, and modify it as it develops, these procedures go back and forth.

To help articulate their ideas, older children may also try to draw some initial designs. The processes associated with woodwork develop the construction knowledge of children. They will eventually join and build in a variety of unique ways in the woodwork.

They find that it is simpler to connect wood parts with flat edges than angled bits. They find out how to make strong and robust connections or how to make their model stand up on its own.

Children become artists, designers, architects, builders, and sculptors as they build.

STEM is a modern learning approach used by science, technology, engineering, the arts, and mathematics as access points to guide student inquiry, dialogue, and critical thinking. Students taking thunderous risks, participate in experiential learning, persist in problem-solving are the final results.

Woodworking with small children is an ideal foundation for STEAM since it connects directly with all STEAM subjects in primary and secondary education. We have to provide true real experiences, not ambiguous alternatives, to allow kids to identify STEAM concepts. Kids build a foundation in their STEAM thinking skills through hands-on learning and are much more likely to acquire an interest in and pursue STEAM subjects so that woodwork could be seen as beneficial to the broader narrative once again.

Woodworking Benefits

These are several advantages of woodworking:

- Eye-hand coordination
- Role-playing
- Independence/self-esteem
- Creative thinking
- Dexterity/fine motor
- Problem-solving
- Imagination
- Stress reliever (pounding)
- Conceptualization
- Comparing/measuring
- Matching/classification
- Sorting
- Textures and properties
- Cooperation
- Increased awareness and Respect for tools and materials
- Understanding of the world around them
- Language development

Developmental Stages of Children's Woodworking:

- Acquaintance with tools and wood
- Simple construction
- Simple skill attempts
- Refinement
- Decorative combinations
- Functional construction
- Emergence of craft

Chapter 2

Development Stages

When most folks think of woodworking for kids, they visualize the final product – perhaps the napkin holder or the birdhouse. But there is much more to a typical woodworking project than the products.

The processes and practices that make up the project steps that are involved.

What Age to Begin

Woodwork shouldn't be for adults and adolescents alone. An excellent way to introduce small children to Woodwork is to explore and practice processes through real tools and processes before anything starts to be constructed. For young children, they must practice their expertise many times to get it going.

It is more important for the new generation than ever to think creatively and develop problematic solutions. Woodwork trains skills such as child-taking and learning through testing and error. It stimulates creative thinking and imagination, which are at least as important as the practical abilities gained in our changing world.

Woodwork includes all aspects of education and development, mathematics support, scientific research, physical coordination, vocabulary, and language to be integral to your curriculum.

Children are initially taught how to be using the tools safely and try techniques properly. With their mastery, pleasure, and pride, they make a visible boost to their self-esteem. Learning continues to progress at the individual pace of each child. After mastering the fundamental skills, they go on open exploration, producing unique creations.

Now they are flourishing their creative thinking and trust in problem-solving when they meet their challenges.

Interestingly, working with instruments leaves a profound memory, which leaves a long-lasting image, even if early children's education is their only woodwork experience.

Education and development

In analyzing Woodwork for children, it is exceptional to see how it includes all training and development sectors and connects the various fields. It covers all the features of effective learning and encourages trusted, creative children with a love of lifelong learning.

Development of personal, social, and emotions

By being valued and trusted, children are empowered. When children are allowed to use real instruments, you gain self - assurance and a sense of commitment. As kids master more equipment and techniques, they are proud to perform more and more complex tasks. This sense of achievement gives children a powerful attitude and a powerful sense of agency and a comprehensive willingness, and the conviction that they can help transform the world around them.

As they continue, children develop continuous attention. Children's concentration is of two levels: first, because of the nature of the tools, children need to concentrate; secondly, because they are motivated to build their wanted project, they are in deep into trouble solving.

Children develop social skills when they discuss and organize a project together. They get to share ideas and learn from others. They learn. "To give children that perception of achievement, the emotional effect of Woodwork lies: 'Yes! I can do that I can do that! 'Experience develops knowledge and skills to strengthen comprehension: a good cycle.

Parents witness happy children, re-enforcing all positive and empowering ethos."

<u>Physical development</u>

Hand-eye coordination is essential for woodworking, and children are increasingly under control because of the development of agility and skill, manipulation, and muscular strength. Fine motor skills (like clamping, screwing) and gross motor skills (like hammering, sawing) are included in Woodwork. (Hammering, sawing). The core strength of children is developed by stirring (sawing, filing), turning (using a screwdriver, drilling, wrench, and vice-pressing), levering (using a claw hammer or a Japanese nail puller), and rubbing (with sandpaper). Tools are part of the physical vocabulary of children's experiences. Besides, children learn about themselves, for example, the importance that safety glasses protect their eyes.

Language and communication

In the woodwork area, a natural discussion is held between adults and children. As wood can be used in innumerable ways, opportunities are discussed thoroughly. Through Experience, children's language of thinking evolves. The children express ideas at the stage of project development, and dialog is ensuing as their plans are reflected and modified. Adults bring new vocabulary to allow children to talk more clearly about their work. The learning of new tools builds awareness-raising skills; children start to listen to instructions carefully.

About Mathematics

Counting is essential for woodworking. Kids measure wood pieces; they have form and weight. Three-dimensional forms build their spatial consciousness. Adults have adequate opportunity to broaden the mathematical knowledge of children, for example, to have them estimate how long a plank of wood must last for a specific purpose.

Many mathematical concepts are linked: classification matches, measurement counts, weight, and size comparisons. Children are intrigued by a cross-section of the age of a tree. Enter into your woodworking area a wide variety of mathematical equipment (rulers, tape-measures, set-squares, spirit levels).

Comprehending the world

It is part of understanding the world to become acquainted with trees and wood. Trees are extremely important for life on our planet, and children are fascinated by learning how and where they are growing.

Even young children begin to acknowledge the connectivity of life with the oxygen that trees and other plants release into the atmosphere. To investigate leaves, branches, and roots, accompany children to the forest if possible. Planting a tree is a great achievement. For example, it is possible to branch out learning by viewing leaves in a clear box, examining different venous structures, leaf prints, and animals living in trees. Talk about wood, where it originates from, and how to uses it. Talk about wood. Research the material of wood. What are its characteristics? It floats, it burns when it is cut, generates sawdust when rubbed, it gets hot.

Explorations

can be diversified – it could be used to make charcoal drawings, for example, after the wood has burned.

Arts and design expression

The main asset of Woodwork is its contribution to the creativity of children. When they create, they become designers, architects, and artists. Avoid setting tasks, such as having each child construct a bird box, but instead encourage them to do what they might like.

This maintains a great deal of excitement and involvement and results in incredibly different ways, ranging from flying hedgehogs to super powerful airplanes.

Creative thinking is a life technique that affects all learning fields. It helps children develop innovative ideas and influence their response to opportunity and setbacks, allowing them to see choices and assess future opportunities.

"Woodwork is an effective tool to develop the critical and creative thinking of children. Children can solve complicated problems and demonstrate their unlimited imaginations with countless opportunities."

Chapter 3
How to Introduce Kids to Woodworking

Few situations are as interesting and challenging as creating something on your own. It is especially true of woodworking and even more thrilling is discovering out that your children have simila desire to create things.

Woodwork is a highly potentially interesting hobby. Once you learn the basics of this craft and master it, the possibilities are limitless. Incorporate this knowledge with teaching your children, and there's something really special about that Experience.

You can not only cultivate a great appreciation for the woodworking craft in your children, but you can also combine many teaching and activity skills without your kid knowing it! Carpentry can help children with their hand and eye coordination, agility, problem-solving, and evaluating skills.

Woodworking can even teach a child how to begin taking an abstract idea from beginning to end and make it genuine through proper planning. Though, when it gets down to working with small children, there's a thin balance between having fun or converting it into a job. Here are eight suggestions on in what ways to introduce your children to woodworking while still creating it a moment for you and your kid to relish.

1. Planning ahead

A few things could dissuade a young kid more than if he doesn't understand what you're doing. While you might want to let your kid know what they're building, plan your line of work before you start, so you don't have to stop reorganizing and search for tools and supplies.

2. Start off slowly

As thrilled as your children are about to start creating and building, continue preparing them slowly. Start introducing the instruments you're going to use to them and also to what you're going to do. You might want to share with them an image of the design when it's completed.

Remember, you would like to start gradually. You wouldn't start by teaching your four-year-old how to utilize a rotary saw. If anything, give small jobs to your younger child. A good job would be to help sand a wooden plank to set it up for staining or allow him or her to measure while holding the ruler and pointing out where the line should start and end.

Begin with the more basic instruments and methods and build on them little by little. A kid's first project could be something as basic as making a set of racks or a small bookshelf.

If you're a teacher, implementing carpentry in your classroom doesn't mean beginning with a full set of Hand tools and power saw tools.

Start easy - a piece of wood and sandpaper; or Styrofoam, golf tees, and a little rubber mallet. From there, a piece of wood with a few screws and a screwdriver can be introduced. Introduce one instrument and one technique at a time.

3. Educate about wood

Incorporate a tree learning unit, wood, and wood uses. Have kids explore the wood – notice the grain, the scent, the feel, the weight, the form differences, etc.

Many different types of wood are available. Educate your children about the various kinds and teach them the significance of the forests and trees and the timber they yield. Try utilizing softwoods like fir, white pine, redwood, or cedar.

Instead of using pine for a project, tell them why you're using oak. Teach your child that woodworking is more important than just cutting and hammering boards together.

Wood can be curved, burnt, carved, painted, stained, or glued to create many distinct and beautiful things. You can show the kitchen cabinets, the furniture in the bedroom, the guitar on the wall, or the picture frame as examples of the wood's versatility.

4. Begin with small projects

It is unrealistic to expect a young kid to assist you construct a dresser, leading to infuriation. It can easily scare your child away from the notion of Woodwork. Proceed by constructing something little with your child so that there is some easy work for your child to do.

5. Use the actual tools

Teach kids the correct use of real tools. Cover the Woodworking Area Rules and clarify that if kids choose not to obey the safety rules, they will have to quit that area and play elsewhere. Safety is always the first and foremost thing! This idea can be learned, as can a healthy appreciation for instruments.

Don't let your kid learn how to make wooden items with toy gadgets. They will be more willing to practice safety when they use real tools. The tools you use are hammers, saws, nails, sandpaper, paintbrushes, paints, or varnishes. Use the simplest saw available, like a hacksaw or cutters that pull and do not need to be pushed. Kids will discover it is a lot easier to use this kind of saw, and it's also safer. Be sure that all your instruments are razor sharp and that they are in proper working order. Sharp instruments get the work done faster and receive more appreciation and trust.

6. Educate your child about equipment safety

Tool safety should be mentioned at the top as safety is extremely important. Teach your children about not only tool safety but moreover to always appreciate the equipment too. Make sure that the screws or clamps are used to keep the wood in its place. You would have to start with nailing for them too. Anticipate and model appreciation for the instruments and the area of woodworking. Learn
and teach children the proper names of all tools. For kids to put the instruments back when they are done with them, trace the instruments' outline on the pegboard. Goggles should be worn at all times

7. Judge when to assist and where to stand aside

While your kid may like to do a good share of the construction, when needed, be present to help. Let the kid do as much as they might do by themselves, but if necessary, make them understand that you are available.

8. Don't be frustrated

You may notice that they'll get bored very easily or would quit quickly, given the age of your children. Don't let that deter you from starting the project. Consider setting a time limit and do not be afraid to take a little break as it will be helpful for both of you. You don't have to finish the whole project in a day.

Equipment and Tools

It is vital to establish a work ethic in your youth early in their lives, but it is equally essential to demonstrate how to love having to learn and learn various talents, and everything starts at home. Kids will still remember the first set of tools they place their hands on and the first thing they learn. Yet, where are you supposed to proceed with all the tools out there?

Woodworking resources:

<u>Wood</u>

Children's choice and creativity need to have various pieces of wood and a plentiful selection. Workshops, sawmills, hardware stores, construction companies, and tree-cutters may assist and provide free off-cuts.

Don't use wood treated with H5 or H4as it can contain arsenic salts, which can be poisonous when converted into sawdust.

If nothing else works, what you can need are 5cm to 11cm thick branches. Compared to furniture grade pinewood, branches that are 5 cm to 11 cm in thickness may be good for sawing easily and easily available. House clearance firms often have damaged tables that they are prepared to get rid of because they are of no value.

Pallets
are frequently free and can quickly be stripped down with a hammer and a pry bar.

For toddlers, fat logs measuring 45cm across and about 26cm – 30cm high can make amazing single workbenches as they can practice by hammering nails on its top.

Though rather softer than regular wood, driftwood is good for learning how to saw. In some areas, it can also be easily found.

Clamps and Bench Vise

Kids don't have the power to hold a wood piece and operate on it with a single hand as adults, so start by teaching them in what ways to use a vice or a G-clip to keep the wood in place.

Some kids may want a little assistance to have the needed clamping force to prevent the wood from moving. Make them tighten up the vice as much as possible, and then apply the last turn to help.

Moving on to the next step, when the wood is securely in place. You can buy vices from carpentry stores, and you should screw them to the work surface so that they don't move. I would advise getting Engineer's vices, as they can be simple to attach to the worktable and avoid the danger of kids sawing on the benchtop. Or, if the reasonable overhang is available on the workbench, a few G clamp vices are a good option. These are relatively cheap and can quickly be shifted - for long planks of wood, two clamps can be put together in a line.

You should show your child how to take action on a desk if you choose to convert a wood dowel into something more. You're going to need a heavy-duty woodworking vise, a 4-inch jaw spread, along an anvil to assist you in getting everything in place. You can utilize this for everything from domestic welding and metal cutting to bar clamping. A swivel base is installed for optimum alignment; the integrated pipe clamp is adjusted for round stock operation.

Measuring tape

Tape measures are cute tools for children. Besides, tape measurements are important instruments around the house. You can use this to teach numbers, and even fractions, to your child. For kids, the measuring tape above is about right. Small hands can reach the lock, and the blade stretches to a useful length for small projects and playing.

Plane Block

You're going to ease the squared edges with a router for pieces touched by people's hands—gates, tables, or anything with a handle. And there's nothing like a children's low-angle block plane and how It is used under adult supervision. Block planes, whose irons split the transparent curls of wood at an angle of 21 degrees, explodes with life lessons. Take apart a little stock at a time, feel the instrument through the job, and work with sharp instruments best. Woodworkers almost always place planes on their side without having to protect the iron edge.

Clothes for Work

Nothing is more attractive and beautiful than a kid prepared to work on a cotton project connected with home improvement and childhood work. The latter is made of a 9-ounce cotton duck of 100% weight with double Knees on the shoulder and elastic braces; the bibs are as large as children.

Pocket for Tools

There are also life lessons in a tool pocket: preparation, selecting the perfect equipment for the project, taking note of your things, but a kid's tool pocket is just plain fun too. This pack of tools comes with hand gear and protective glasses. It is even easier to walk into the store and produce screwdrivers, pliers, paper scales, and a wrench. A child who handles his own gear, however, becomes a much more willing supporter.

Nails and hammers

Adults may be afraid that kids will hit each other if they allow them to have hammers. But there is also a risk of children hitting other kids with other items, such as blocks and toys from the corner of the block box or balls from the ball pit. In the case of oversight, it is essential watching over the kids and ensuring that hammers (and other equipment) are applied for the intended purposes.

Talk to kids about raising the hammer lower than their head's height for safety reasons, which prevents them from accidentally striking themselves or any other child that is standing behind them. Kid (or Small) hammers can be bought from carpentry stores. It is an affordable and easy exercise to shorten a wooden-handled hammer of standard length, needing only a plain saw.

Tell students how to use their wrist and swing the hammer to strike the nail and explain it. As the child gains confidence after using the short hammer, they can start to hold the nail on their own to get in full swing.

When kids have perfected to start a nail in a piece of scrap wood, a full-size hammer can be given with a little more instruction. If necessary, a clothing peg holding the base of the nail will be useful in ensuring small fingers from accidentally getting hurt.

When choosing nails, avoid the impulse to select cheap panel nails as they easily bend over. Long nails can go out through the wood damaging the underlying surface or bench. Clouts are inexpensive and perfect in length.

Try other sizes too, when the kids are familiar

with clouts. Avoid large nails because they are crafted to be placed in with a hammer heavier than a kid can handle.

The remodeler 12-ounce hammer, shown above, is the perfect woodwork for the child. But at 12 oz., the item is as small as it can be and as easy to control. Kids like to bang on stuff, so why not create a board with a few nails inside it and let them hammer it? And when they're performed, you're going to take back the excellent hammer so that they might not destroy or outgrow and utilize it for their own ventures.

Screws and screwdrivers

A small crosshead screwdriver (fat one) for small hands works just fine. A power-driven screwdriver could be a great add on, but they typically take ample to charge, like electrical drills.

Kids Cordless Drill

Don't ever use a drill with small kids that is powered by mains. There is too much torque in mains powered drills; and also, there is a hazard of hair and clothes getting caught and snarled, sustaining major injuries.

They are, at times, referred to as Gimlets. They lack the strength of a hand brace and the rpm of the egg beater hand drills, but they really do seem to work well, particularly in greenwood.

Children have many drills for toys. The thing is that they are only children. It could be best to reevaluate a practical device when your kids have outgrown the use of pretend tools. A familiar example is a drill, but then you can choose some impact driver for your kid.

There are the following reasons why kids should have a certain impact driver:

Suitable for smaller hands

<u>Low voltage</u>

No big wedge with big gaps, a robust textured ring – and more secure No tightening requires high strength. It allows a fast connector to be used. Switching bits back and forth

It is an instrument that they will grow with, and not a toy is thrown away later. Although it's enticing to buy the child's favorite color matching one, you can get one of the tools you might have on the battery site/service. If you don't have a product preference, then go for their preferred color.

Such devices are also battery-free or battery-size available. It is safer to continue with small batteries such as 1.5 or 2 AA because they are all lightweight and lower in capacity. As a matter of fact, they're also inexpensive.

Not only can buying a driver of real impact develop their abilities, but it also makes sure that it can be moved to the mom or dad's workshop for use once they lose attractiveness.

Cordless drills are usually used for drilling the holes and screws. Many of the cheap 12-volt ones do not have a lot of power. A 12-volt cordless drill can be used fairly competently by some preschoolers, but observation is important again. If necessary, a grown-up should be in close vicinity of the child to provide for the child's safety. At the bottom of the handle, cordless drills are quite heavy, which neutralizes the torque. It also has a clutch system that generally allows some control on the force applied.

They also ensure keyless buckles with lesser areas where things can be pulled in – however,
when using tools and especially drills, long hair (for girls and boys and adults) must always be pushed back into the ponytail.
A hand drill is the other category of the drill. Different kinds are generally available plastic, one with a twisty handle on the side that appears to be a regular electrical drill and one that is geared and made from metal. The one of metal is the stronger model, but for smaller children, it is rather large and therefore difficult (although most 5 to 7-year-olds won't have any difficulty with it). The plastic drill is all right, but it may not only last long. The metal one is

capable of taking bigger drill bits.

The wood must be held with a clamp or vice for protection when using the drill since a drill, whether electric or by hand, takes two hands.

Use a larger bit of drill. Approximately 11mm is the maximum that most kids can manage to pierce a part of 12mm thick pine. Usually, an 8mm to 9mm bit is ideal. Educational providers usually sell 3mm to 5mm bits, although the larger drill bit takes advantage of resisting sideways by forcing children to wear them. Sometimes wire nails are used as inexpensive drill bits, but they don't work that well. Kids may try to hit the nails with their drills, so stay prepared to sharpen the drill about one time a month in the school or 3-6 months in home-based learning. If you select plastic drills, then you will often need to substitute them. Metal drills generally come with a warranty of a lifetime. A cheap wireless drill is suggested, but not extremely important.

4-in-1 Mat Tool

The 4-in-1 tool available on the market consists of 4 electrical tools for woodworking combos:

- Drilling Press
- Sander Disk
- Lathe
- Screw jigsaw

Generally speaking, it's quiet and efficient for a little machine. Your kid will love to shape the block of wood's segments on the lathe together with the thin plywood sheets provided in the package, to be cut and sanded.

Children's tool belts

The workshop's time is connected to skills learning, and a part is also a little dress-up. Children tend to imitate grown-ups. They love doing what their parents do and wearing what their parents wear. Of course, your tool belt, however partially mounted, wouldn't fit your child's waist. Everything comes off instantly. So much to carry that he/she ends up sporting it in both hands. It will become a safety apprehension after a couple of minutes as the child has no hands to safeguard himself.

A children's bench hook

The goal of woodworking is to assist young children in making things

from wood, a natural resource. Thus, a beneficial bench hook can aid achieve this goal and help children do various things.

• It can help children to saw more precisely. There is no denying that accurate cuts offer a good shape and look at completed projects. Success promotes confidence and pride, of course.

• A bench hook for children will help them to saw more easily. It will

• A safe tool that will not lead to any type of accident when properly utilized and will keep children's hands safe.

PVA adhesive

Paper (to be used for decorations, sails, making pictures frame)

Water-based paint and brush

Bottle tops of plastic milk (make great lights and wheels), string (pullstrings to attach to children's toys, for guitar strings.), and anything for décor or other purposes, like foil, fake fur, cloth scraps, leaves, and even feathers!

Get a socket set for kids to make stuff with bolts and nuts. To toughen bolts more effectively than using spanners, kids can practice with the socket set.

Plier

Pliers are usually used to pick things up and pull things out. Pliers are quite close to scissors as the child gets used to utilizing them like tweezers to pick up things.

Do not get pliers with cutters because if you catch your finger, these could be dangerous. Small electric pliers are the right size for kids and are widely available. They are about half size of the engineering pliers and are best suited for small hands.

A child's workbench

It is unnecessary to provide a dedicated workbench for woodworking, but a child requires a table surface of some kind (kids cannot do sawing and some of the stuff they want to do on the floor). A workbench is necessary for early childhood centers to ensure that all equipment and wood are kept next to each other and easy to access. Up to four children can use a 1200mm x 600mm workbench safely, depending on the task that children are doing – for example, if they are gluing and not sawing, more kids are more likely to mount

on the bench. The bench should be around the waist height for the children who use it.

Parents ought to invest in a decent workstation because a good worktable is incredibly important for a happy, secure, and safe workshop experience with kids. The following attributes should be used for a good workbench:

- Storage of goods
- Holes of dogs
- Configured rack
- Big surface of work

You may have noticed that there is no presence of a vise. The purpose should be to teach children how to properly lock their work, as it helps avoid frustration and accidents.

Saws for children

The ideal way to teach kids how to make things is by sawing boards —safely. Maybe it's not the safest option to give them a 15-pound worm drive, but a small, flexible Japanese-style pull-saw. You can consider hand saws that have super-primo and not-so-pricey replaceable blades. They cut with the pulling stroke, which is much easier than the push stroke cutting.

And they're sharp, with no danger. Plus, you're going to be able to use them when your kid doesn't need them. They're perfect for all kinds of projects. Before your kid is prepared to practice the handsaw, protection has to be the main condition.

The wood should be secured with a handy miter box, clamps, or bolts. Children will be advised to place both hands or one behind the back of the saw. These will remove almost any possible accidents that might occur during the sawing phase.

With that, the next step is to prepare a saw that's just right for your child. There are very few options to choose from, as with every woodworking tool choice.

Hack Saw:

Hack saws made for metal cutting are the best starting saw for children. The teeth of the saw are not too hostile and thin. It makes it stress-free to launch quickly and go to and fro. The structure of teeth is to hold up a decent amount of mishandling and offer a fairly decent cut. The blade isn't quite large, and that doesn't get as easily lodged inside the wood like the traditional wood saw. The saw's sharp edge can be turned over as an additional incentive and can be adjusted to cut the stroke of the push or the stroke of the pull. Make sure you find one with tension at both ends of the blade, not those that are weak where the blade edge is not protected. Extra blades are fairly readily available and affordable. When they're ready to operate real wood saws, this saw can be used to serve its real objective of metal cutting, and it's going to be an instrument that will last all their lives.

Pull saws:

Pull-saws are available in many sizes and shapes, with teeth cut on a pulling stroke. Typically, teeth are finer than conventional saws, so the edges are sharper, which means that cutting is quicker and easier for them. Carpenter-type saws are advised for use as they have one side of the teeth. With one edge designed for rip-cut, whereas the other side designed for cross-cutting, double-sided saws are pretty useful. Still, the existence of pointed teeth on either side of the edges presents a little extra health hazard for youngsters. The one setback to the pull saw is that its sharp teeth can be broken relatively quickly if it is ill-used.

Kids Toolbox Saws:

Kid's toolbox saws have a tougher blade and are short that makes them generally very durable. The plastic handle lets it appear as a toy saw, but that's not true. Both the pull -and- push movement cut the wood so that it cuts quickly and efficiently. The blade shield is protected, and the teeth are completely covered, the children are shielded by those who violently pick up their devices and remove them. It's a nice little saw for children.

Coping Saws:

Kids should better avoid handling jigsaws or coping saws. When Kids use them, the blades sometimes bind and crack. It requires more time than their parents to understand and learn how to use these saws and a more cautious hand to work with them. It's a Mistake made by most parents for starting their children with coping saws as they may seem small and easier for the children, but neither of the saws shown above is a safer option.

Children Workshop Protection

While a toolset comes with a range of tools, parents should be sensible enough to start introducing single tool at a particular time for their children. One tool may be introduced after seven days or more.

In this way, it is much easier to focus on the function and teach children about tools' safety. Let us now go through the strict guidelines for handling saws effectively and safely:

• Children need hold the saw hands with both of their hands.

• Children should only saw on wood that is secure in the vise. They can saw the wood in the miter box, too.

Sawing on the furniture will not be allowed.

There are some instruments in the collection that need not be used for a long period of time before you think that the device is suitable for the child's age, behavior, and skill.

Final Word on the Saws

Whatever the type you've chosen for your kid, it's imperative for children and parents to realize that any type of sawing is really a tender act. Most kids acquire the incorrect impression when they see their adults in an offensive, powerful act of sawing, that the more you thrust forward, the quicker you work. The harder you saw, the easier it is to cut. They're both wrong. A saw must be pushed gently and also gently pulled to let the sharp teeth do the job. The saw ought to

be held softly, not stiffly. The basic idea is that if something is clenched (hands, butt, and teeth) while you're sawing, something is wrong with your method of sawing.

Tool Box Step-Tool

The Step N Stack-On toolbox will help your kid balance it when working on the worktable and then put his equipment inside when it's over.

They are larger than the regular size toolbox that are appropriately planned to be comfortable for children or adults, particularly when standing above it. It is estimated that it will carry as much as 325lbs. These stacks up just fine, so you should buy more of them.

Additionally, your kid may even use it like a worktable and a bench as a toolbox and step stool.

<u>Additional accessories</u>

Sandpaper – cut the sandpaper in half or quarters to make it feasible for children. Provide rough, coarse, smooth sandpaper. Ruler – either a folding ruler or a long rigid ruler. It is possible to introduce the measurement handy for drawing lines on flat wood and older children who can recognize numbers.

Carpenter's pencil – children may draw a dot or a cross to mark where they hammer in a nail. For other purposes, such as demonstrating where to begin sawing, pencil marks can also be used.

Children are young for particular tools.

You will must have a collection of furniture-safe play tools so that children can have fun with those tools in spaces where the actual tools are not suitable, such as inside the car, inside the living area, or at the home of your grandma.

They involve freedom to explore while not being monitored and instructed; with a screwdriver, no hammering, no playing with a saw, no sticking a drill inside the mouth, etc.

There are tons of tools that you can choose the best for your child. Some of them are more accurate than others. Those who look more genuine do not hold up and generate some kind of confusion about real and a toy. They're going to play because it's a gift, they can't play if it's not a gift, or they shouldn't play.

There are a variety of instrument sets for children. Both vary in the objects they contain and in the worth of the items. You can purchase a single tool at one time that is an adult tool but accessible to kids. They're often prepared a little stronger, and they're intended more for performance than for some play, so they just work better when used.

Teach Children to Use These 10 Basic Tools

1. Tape Measure

Kids are acquainted with numbers depending on their age and like to use this new expertise. An excellent way to learn to read the tape measure is to measure items around the house, and the extra calculation and subtraction exercise never goes in vain.

2. Screwdriver

Screws can help secure many joints for beginners, and knowledge about the variety of screws will enable a kid to take apart many things. I've found a great process in seeing how things are built is to take things apart, which screwdrivers excel at.

3. Block Planes

A little block plane won't be a kid's shop workhorse, but they're going to love using one. Creating shavings is a thing that is loved by adults, and children are also no different. Cutting away sharp corners and flatting boards just to make shavings are fun tasks with the plane grasped with two hands.

4. Clamps

Clamps are as helpful to children as adults, from holding a piece a kid is working on to pull together a newly molded joint. It is good to learn to know which size and type of clamp to use and how to apply it.

5. Pencil

Although your child has undoubtedly been using writing tools for years, do they really know how to handle them exactly?

Understanding how to define an exact line and how important a pointed pencil is, are essential abilities. I prefer a mechanical pencil a lot.

6. Vise

Same as clamps, a vise is irreplaceable for securing woodwork properly while it is being labored on. Small hands aren't powerful, and a vise makes it much trouble-free for tough work to be done.

7. Hammer

The hammer is a basic instrument found in many hardware stores with nails, assembling, tapping into dowels, and so much more. It is

best to find a small child-sized hammer.

8. 4" Square

Although they will soon not be carving advanced joints by hand, children should understand how to operate a square and what it can do. It may also lead to parallel, perpendicular, etc., geometry discussions, all of which are generally a part of life and woodworking.

9. Drill (cordless)

Their first powered tool, a small drill, low-powered, helps drill small holes, counter-sinking, use driving screws, and dowels. It is surely

not the first tool I will instruct my child to use but introducing power to the balance will surely open their eyes. Additional esteem must be applied.

10. Hand Saw

I mainly use Japanese saws in my workshop, which I will teach my children to use. I discovered that, if your upper body has sufficient strength and is self-assured in operating it, a saw of Western-style creates problems for some people. On the contrary, a western-style saw is a little stronger and forgiving.

Chapter 4
How to familiarize tools to kids`

A good way to get in progress is by putting out one sort of tool at a time for a couple of days or a few weeks (based upon the frequency of use). This practice makes it easier to teach the kids how to use each tool relatively safe and simpler as, at the same time, you can show several kids together. Before you incorporate more tools, wait until the kids have developed confidence with the instruments and safely use the tools.

It is vital to consider what needs to be done if you have to leave the working area. At all times, the area has to be under close supervision.

Chapter 5

How to Use Tools

The most important part is that real tools should be used. Plastic instruments do not teach kids how to manipulate a real instrument accurately.

<u>Clamps</u>

These are the essential tools in woodworking that you will use. Clamps are your good friend when it comes to protection and safety. There are many kinds of vices and clamps; get to know as many kinds as you can and their uses.

"C" clamp is the simplest clamp you will experience. It is a good tool to temporarily attach a piece of wood to some surface, freeing up your hand so that you can concentrate on your instrument and task.

Tools for Shaping:

<u>Sandpaper</u>

Sandpaper is one of the kid's best introductory tools when it comes to woodwork. Most children find the texture itself intriguing. Its aim is obvious when children are demonstrated that it is possible to use sandpaper to change the form of a piece of wood.

An incredibly engaging activity would be to let children sand pieces of scrap wood.

To help kids get a better grip while using it, tie a piece of sandpaper around over a block of wood.

Clamp the scrap wood piece to a surface to encourage children to concentrate on the back-and-forth sanding action.

Sandpaper produces a lot of dust, so after you're done, be sure to sweep.

Tools for Attachment:

Hammers

Hammer is the tool used to put together materials, often wood.

Find smaller young children's hammers.

Explain the hammer parts first, like the handle allows you to swing it, the nail is hit by the flat end, and the claw (that is sharp) pulls out nails from the wood.

Convey kids how to grasp a hammer properly.

Let them exercise nail hammering into soft pieces of scrap wood (similarly an old stub of tree works terrific). Patience is always the key. Children can get irritated when the nails end up crooked. Tell them that training helps and show them.

How to hammer in nails without striking your thumb is the chief concern as it is unavoidable to strike your thumb with a hammer while using the nail and hammer. Choose a simple clothespin to hold the nail near its edge instead with of your fingers. You will be holding the clothespin, and that will be holding the nail, so you won't hit your fingers even if you don't hit the nail, enabling kids to use a hammer on their own to practice.

Screwdriver

Screwdrivers are often used to attach wood by turning the screw into the material. It can be quite challenging to push and turn a screwdriver while also maintaining it steady, and it takes a lot of time for the kids to master.

Explain to kids what the screwdrivers can do

Demonstrate different screwdrivers and screws and how different screwdriver shapes and sizes correspond to different types of screws.

Try using a screwdriver with a piece of rigid Styrofoam or Polystyrene that can be found in most home depot or hobby stores. Driving screws into this type of material is a little easier than into wood, so kids can force the screws in and take them out again and again. Let children exercise turning and pushing the screws into a softwood after you learn the Styrofoam exercise.

Tools for Prepping:

Drill

By using various sizes of drill bits, a drill can make a range of holes in wood. Two types of drills that exist are power drills, hand drills, and. It is very necessary to describe to kids that drill bits in any form can be very sharp and need to be handled with care. Hand drills are of many styles: a very robust and efficient model is the 'egg-beater' drill, and it is a great tool to explore

• Using a hand drill may require one-on-one help and support with each child; this should be considered when educating tools in a large group.

You first lock the wood in place to use a hand drill. Mark On the wood with a pencil, where you need a hole and how large it should be. Let kids discover drilling holes in scrap wood; make sure they also try out various sizes of bits. The practice is important, as with all the other instruments.

Be careful that unwanted holes are not drilled into a workbench or floor.

• Safety Note: With young children, don't use a power drill. For quick

fixes or to assemble stuff for your students or kids to explore, a teacher or parent may find a power drill is essential.

Tools for Cutting:

Saws

Saws are tools that are important in woodwork. They are sharp and can be dangerous, but they can also be quite helpful when correctly used.

Guidance and safety are extremely significant when using a saw with a small person.

Stress At all times, to keep your fingers far from the blade.

Use a small coping saw for young children as it is lightweight and well balanced.

Be sure to clamp your wood off the edge of a table at all times. While the kid is sawing, t the wood should be moving around.

Keep both hands on the handle during the sawing process. A child would take a long time and a lot of persistence to saw through a piece of wood. The payoff is that the kid can modify a piece of wood physically in a significant way. Turning a piece of wood into two can be pretty exciting.

When you start to practice using a saw, be sure to use fairly thin and soft pieces of wood.

Chapter 6
The Safety System

An essential element of woodworking is safety. Safety is the key whether you are 4 or 40 years old.

<u>Keep dangerous instruments off-limits.</u>

Most power tools are dangerous, too heavy, and for young kids to be used by themselves, other than lightweight drills and scroll saws. When you are not around, placing locks on electricity plugs prevents them from getting used. Also, keep sharp hand tools like chisels and utility knives locked in tool chests.

<u>Make eye protection a habit of work.</u>

If working with any tool, always wear safety r glasses or goggles. Goggles come in different adult and children's sizes, so buy a pair that fits every child well and won't fall off when working.

Like safety straps in a car, safety glasses should be compulsory for any child before picking up a tool. Set a great example by sporting your own safety goggles.

<u>Dress right.</u>

Roll up the long sleeves, tuck in the tails of the shirt, and button up the front of the shirt so that clothes are not caught at work. Tie back the long hair for safety purposes and visibility. When planning to work in the shop, wear protective boots or closed-toe shoes.

Supervise the use of tools.

Keep an eye on him until you are sure that a child has a fine grasp over a tool and understands the correct safety procedures, whenever a tool is used, have a fully equipped first aid kit with you in the shop if an accident occurs,

Show how tools are to be carried correctly.

Tools must be carried with blades or bits pointing down and far from the body, just like scissors. Teach kids to lay down the tools when they are not using them and never run with an instrument in hand.

Minimize your distractions.

iPad, animals, and little children running around take attention away from the job at hand and raise the risk of a mishap. An untidy shop is also a hindrance and a danger if equipment can be knocked off the walls, benches or. Sweep up the sawdust to avoid slipping.

Use softwoods.

For children to cut, drill, sand, and shape their own, hardwoods such

as oak, maple, and ash can be difficult. They're going to have a smoother time working with pine, poplar, and cedar, to name a few.

Cushioning hammer blows.

Children seem to appreciate hammering nails innately. A kid will have better control over a hammer that is lightweight (about 10 ounces or less) than a little "kid's hammer" Like the Thumb saver, a magnetic nail holder that keeps fingers safe from mistaken blows, and even a tennis ball pinned on the hammer's claw end protects painful collisions on the backswing with the child's head.

Clamp the piece of work.

It's too hard to hold woodwork and also a tool for small hands. Stable the work with a clamp or a vise so that both hands could be on the tool.

Start with a small handsaw

If you permit your child to actually use a handsaw, please make sure it's slightly short, fine-toothed sharp, and. It is easier to start with Japanese, pull-type saws that are less likely to snag and have more than 12 teeth per inch. Warn children always do work with both hands on the handle, which gives better control and helps to keep fingers aside from the teeth, so please ensure the saw's handle is large enough for a dual grip.

11. Lower the working table

Kids need a working surface that is positioned at a good level to have proper control of their instruments and efficiently see what they're doing.

Keep the cleaning in mind.

Select water-based paints, stains, and adhesives. They are much easier to clean than solvent-based substances (as long as you clean them off before they dry out). (As long as you wash them off before they dry). (As long as you wash them off before they dry). They're safer, too.

Steady and slow

Another significant safety aspect is patience. Don't rush off the steps. It can take quite a long time for a woodworking project.

Ordered Workspace

To avoid missteps and interruptions, have a clean and orderly workspace. You also can work directly on the ground instead of at a table when discovering woodwork with very young kids.

Safe attitude and rules for discussing and reminding children as needed

Do not ever run holding the tools.

No instruments above head height.

Use each of the tools correctly.

Do not remove tools from the area of the workbench.

Chapter 7
Tool Techniques

You can begin to show them what each of the tools will do after a safety discussion with your child about woodworking and its tools. Some would like to start with simple jobs such as timber sanding or drill holding. But you and your kid need to decide on what type of project you want to work on together before you begin.

There's a lot you can construct that's actually going to come in pretty useful, or that's going to be fun for your kid after you create it, such as a rocking wooden horse, a Barbie dollhouse, a simple tree house, or a cart car.

Once you select a project, you can convey your child what tools are needed for the job and why. Have them pass you each instrument, making sure they know each one by the proper name, so they can gain knowledge while watching. You can make them help them out a little more by helping them decide and do a few steps after they fully understand how you are utilizing each of the wood tools.

You might not want to give them access to use a saw or drill based on their age. A suitable age would be 10 when the kids are a bit less clumsy and can understand the aspects of the risk that tools can pose.

For your smaller kids, another option is to start with a child-sized tool kit.

By providing them this kit, it is going to give them the courage and determination to help you. It is very inspiring for them to have their very own toolkit. For example, if you make a wooden rack for hanging keys or coats, you drill the hole, and your child can place the hooks in them. You can also allow them to put all the pieces together or fill in the small holes you drill.

The real fun starts after finishing the project. Bring the painting tools out and enjoy fun and creativity in a family moment. As most kids love to decorate with color schemes, this should be positioned in the child's hands. If this is their first painting job, you can teach them how to smoothly brush the paint in the same direction onto the wood.

And let them pick the colors and where they're going.

Congratulate them when the project is fully complete! Make them realize that it was their job that made the timber what it is now. This will open a door of possibilities o for them to wish new things to be created. They may even come up with some award-winning invention; you never know!

Getting to know your equipment

Who isn't a little pleased for getting a fresh shiny hammer? And who would not feel such a little inspired after drilling a tiny hole into an otherwise, sturdy board successfully? They almost instinctively realize what they are for when children first see hammers. If they are lucky and nails and wood are available, as well as eager parents who might allow them to keep driving nail after nail, experimenting with different ways of pulling the crooked ones out and trying several methods to maintain a wiggly board still A few parents, noting that instruments can be bulky, sharp, as well as a bit dangerous, do not allow their kids access to woodworking tools.

We hope to provide enough ideas, provide ample good advice, and generate enough excitement with this book to enable children and parents to learn basic carpentry skills.

First, this book provides you with knowledge and advice for using the instruments to become your reliable buddies and carpentry companions. We have given safety tips and working advice for each instrument; read this section first!

Hammering

The most fundamental carpentry activity is to push a nail into two pieces of woods to attach them together. And the hammer alone is perhaps the most fundamental instrument for carpenters. r Your hammer not only lets you pound nail after nail, but it also serves as a pry bar, a tool to dig, a hatchet, or your own arm's useful extension.

Momentum is the first step to hammering. Through the swing of your hand, shoulder, elbow, wrist, and the gathering energy you will generate is what powers your hammer's blow. Imagine that at the end of a string, you are swinging a weight. While you could catch the weight in your hands and strike the object directly with it, the blow would be even better if you could stack up all the forces needed to swing it in the arc. The further your hold is from the hammer's head, the more power you can get from each hit. Although also guiding the

swing, you can grip the hammer as much further from the head as you can handle.

The second secret to performance in hammering is hard striking. Most of the hammer strike's force goes into convincing the nail to resolve the wood fibers' own inertia and significant resistance. If pushing a nail through a slice of pine needs 50 pounds of energy, so all the 46-pound blows in the universe won't make the nail budge. It is impossible to believe that a 10-pound hit is far more powerful than a dozen major 52-pound blows.

This theory also occurs when you start nails. Many people swing carefully, afraid that they could strike their fingertips instead of their nails.

Many ineffective taps and a larger number of chances of hitting some fingertips are the result. Place the nail securely, target carefully, and strike like you mean it when it comes to hammering. The nail is going to realize you mean business.

Bending

A bended nail is the consequence of the hammer's swing that does not fully fit with the nail's shank. To prevent bending a nail, have a close look at where the nail is pointed, and aim to bring the swing down as if it were going to reach the point across the top of the nail and through the shank. You can straighten it with the claw of the hammer if you bent a nail and then drive it again, but it is likely to bend again. It is typically best to take the bent nail out and start the same hole with a fresh nail.

Crooked nail

The misdirected or crooked nail is another occasional hammering mishap. Take it out and begin anew if the nail does not go where you need it to be. But don't place your nail again in the same hole. It will only convince your nail that you want the same mistaken direction to be taken. Begin the nail in a new place instead. And then a trick is more on its own, digging out a nail. Your hammer claw will be used for this. Slide the claw under the nail head such that in the V of the claw, the nail shank lies. Under the hammer, place a block of wood; the block will provide you with greater strength to pull the nail and shield the workpiece from injury. Keep tightly down the floor, grab on the end of its hammer handle, and draw back the handle toward you.

Do not feel guilty if, from time to time, you have had to pull out a nail.

Look at the instrument in your hand closely, and you 'will see that it was made to pull nails almost as well as to push them in

Using a set of nails

Some designs involve a finished surface - one which is not disturbed by a nail head design. A nail set is a little basic instrument that allows you to place a nail head flat with or below the piece's surface; it is the easiest way to do this. Setting a nail means that the nail's head is firmly pulled against the wood, enhancing its staying strength. To use a set of nails, grip the body with your other hand. Set the end on the nail head that you intend to sink and connect the body with the nail shaft (this is the nail shaft).

It can be a bit difficult and sometimes requires guesswork). Hold the nail firmly, look carefully, and with the hammer, strike the tip of the instrument squarely. Check the effect, reposition the package of nails, and strike it.

And again. Proceed until the head of the nail is sunk well below the top of the wood.

Sawing

Alignment is the secret to making every hand saw work. A saw would slide through the kerf it has produced in a piece of wood if correctly lined up, with just the cutting teeth opposing the carpenter's drive. If the saw continues to bind along the cut's sides, it may become more difficult to push, and it could become hard to cut completely! The added strain of a saw that keeps binding can wear you out, and the extra pressure you will have to employ will make the saw edge more likely to come out of the groove, which can be risky. So, keep your alignment focused!

Begin by positioning your body to use your saw properly: Assuming you're right-handed,

Stand your left foot before your right foot, nearly opposite to your board. For successful sawing, your right arm ought to be able to travel back

and forth easily around your body.

To stabilize the board, you're cutting with your left hand, hold your fingertips far away from the city. If you're left-handed, standing in the same direction, but with your right foot in front of your left and steadying the board with your right hand.

Your arm, elbow, hand, and saw should be lined together while you push and pull the saw to create the cut. A slow, even stroke is better. You may want to do a few warm-up movements; before adding the saw, let the saw pass in the air over the board in a completely straight line.

Dragging it over the top of the board is a complication.

By placing the saw teeth on the wood, resting his thumbnail against the blade, and pulling the saw carefully in the reverse direction of the cutting motion of the saw, a carpenter will begin a cut (toward himself for a push saw or away from himself for a pull saw). For the first few strokes, the thumb stays on the board as a reference until a groove in the wood has developed.

Because this approach leaves fingers in extreme danger, we came up with a better family woodworking technique. A slice of scrap wood is clamped against the line that we intend to cut. We then draw the blade towards this guidance before a deep groove has been carved in the blade's wood. In reality, for the whole cut, the guide block may be left in position. It maintains the saw blade perfectly balanced before the work is completed, prevents crooked hits, and improves young carpenters' enjoyment in their tasks.

Using a jigsaw

Jigsaw is the most realistic form of saw to cut into a curved path (like

the figure of a wave an animal shape or). (Like the outline of an animal shape or a wave). (Like the outline of an animal shape or a wave). At first, some children are hesitant to use the jigsaw, but they soon get, Well, the grasp of it. They become so proud of themselves because they were really proud of themselves.

They believe they have perfected it. First of all, always mark the cutting line to don't want to build when cutting; a complete focus on

cutting would be needed.

The bottom of the jigsaw's front plate is called the soleplate, and it resembles the foot of the sewing machine. Through the plate, the blade goes up and down. When you are about to cut, the soleplate's forward side lies on the panel with the sharp blade not touching wood yet. To launch the saw, pull the lever, and when it is working smoothly, guide it through the cut. The saw must quickly break through the wood; for the jigsaw to achieve steady progress, you do not have to exert any strain. Steer gently and deliberately, holding the soleplate smooth against the wood, directing the saw blade all along the line you've marked. If you have drawn a line that bends too strongly for the saw blade to follow, aim to back it up just a little and slash into the inside edge of the kerf. You allow the blade more room to pivot by expanding the seam in this manner.

To finish the cut, you will have to perform the process many times.

Do not attempt to force a sudden turn on the blade; turning the blade

sharply will not help make the turn and snap off the blade. Finally, when working the jigsaw, note to use protective glasses, as you do while using any and every power tool.

Drilling

Drilling creates a hole by pushing something heavy against the surface and turning it around and around till it goes right through. Although the idea could be simple, before you move on converting anything in reach into Swiss cheese, you must bear a couple of things in mind.

Tidbits and Bits

There are as many various kinds of drill bits as there are holes that need drilling. However, this book's activities need just "twist" pieces, bits of Forstner, and countersink bits.

What you possibly think of as regular drill bits are "Twist" bits. They are used in this book for certain projects, and the required scale is often noted.

With smooth bottoms and, sides the Forstner bits build gaps. Instead, you can use paddle bits that cost less, but they start to bind and jam and produce a rougher hole.

Despite the extra cost, we opt for utilizing the Forstners.

The countersink bit creates a hole at the top with a tapered recess. When you are pre-drilling for a screw and want it to be flush with not protruding from the wood surface, the recess is needed.

At the lumber supply shop, you can find Fuller bits. Those bits have a shaft. They create a hole that fits a certain wood screw size and countersinks the screw in one process. Fuller parts are not required since we will use drywall screws in this book for projects.

Make your mark

A pencil dot is not the easiest way to locate the position you are going to drill holes. A pencil dot can be challenging to locate later if you map drilling holes in advance because it does not precisely mark the drilling location. Draw crosshairs instead- make two small perpendicular lines whose junction marks the exact place where you're going to rill.

Method of Drilling

It is important for simple drilling - and that is what this book asks for - to keep the drill as straight and firm as possible. Keep the bit balanced vertically while you are drilling vertically down through a slice of wood. Hold the bit horizontally balanced while you're drilling from the side.

Apply constant pressure as you drill to avoid the bit moving further into the wood. Using your right hand to twist the handgrip on a brace drill or pull the lever on a power drill, if you are right-handed, use the left hand to press. Do the opposite if you're left-handed.

Through leaning into the drill, you will employ your body weight to support your drive. Just make sure that the drill is not moved further from this

vertical or horizontal orientation.

Most notably, maintain eyes focus at all moments on the job at hand (through protective goggles, of course).

Keeping bits clean

When you have a power drill, the bit often gets blocked and keeps progressing through the timber. Remove it from the hole if this occurs. With the drill constantly running, clean the dust from the gap and the bit. Wait until the drill finishes spinning, remove the accumulated sawdust from the groove in the bit with the tip of a screw or nail if the sawdust doesn't slip out when you take the bit out of the cavity. Be cautious: it may be quite hot!

If you are using a Forstner bit, operate the drill at a steady pace such that it easily slices through the wood. Nice helical shavings will build up around the growing hole with the right velocity. Drilling too hard would only scrub across the bottom of the hole's cutting edge and heat up and dull the piece.

Usage of Bores and Bits

The brace is one of the earliest kinds of hand-powered drills. You employ a brace including a self-feeding bit that has a pointing screw on the tip. The screw twists when you turn the brace knob, pushing the bit's cutting edge through the wood.

To use a brace, place your weak hand on the wide round top handle and force it down while spinning the handgrip with the other hand. With your upper side, you can create more energy by pressing your chest against it. (Two handgrips and a smooth surface for the chest to drive against certain early braces were originally designed.) Sustain constant pressure against the support. Otherwise, the screw would strip out (meaning it will pull out of the wood, taking with it the
wood fibers needed to hold it in place).

The brace is the best tool for two children to operate together, one gripping and leading and the other winding around the brace with both arms. It is one of the safest cutting tools with its slow-moving speed, and its strong leverage allows it a decent option for turning broad bits of Forstner. A brace chuck can normally hold normal drill bits, but it's not just meant for them; therefore, you can use this method for several drilling activities.

Usage of Power Drill

Using a power drill is pretty straightforward if you get the basic drilling principles down as long as you are careful. With your weaker hand, grip the drill's body and pull the lever with your stronger hand.

As with all power equipment, children using power drills should be monitored. There are two simple dangers of utilizing a power drill: One unintentionally creating a hole where a hole is not needed, such as in a tabletop, the porch board, or someone's finger. The other more significant danger is that the bit or chuck gets wrapped around a sleeve or a lock of hair. Remember, even at a reasonably slow pace, a power drill spins at hundreds of rotations per minute.

Therefore, the first rule to use a power drill is No dangling ends. If your hair is long, tie it. If your sleeves are long, turn them up, and don't leave ends floppy. A similar possibility is that the drill bit will tie up and stop spinning. Suddenly, the drill itself will perform all the spinning, which will bend the wrist very forcefully around it.

Therefore, the second rule: constantly hold a tight grasp on the drill.

You must have one hand on the drill's grip and the other on the body in certain cases. Bear in mind that it is more probable to tie up a larger diameter bit than a smaller one, and a paddle bit is much more likely to send a yank to the wrist than a bit of Forstner.

A binding drill bit will cause the piece you are drilling to swing abruptly into action. You must obey rule three to avoid this: Clamp your piece of work firmly.

Drill parts are specifically hardened such that a sharp point can be preserved. Consequently, they are more fragile than other steel forms, and they may break into sharp, flying bits when they are bent. The first time our kids interacted with a power tool, they flexed their pieces and almost split them.

And this refers to rule four: If you use a power drill, wear eye safety. And the last rule: When they are not in operation, unplug all the power tools. Meaning that once you have cloned a hole, the plug comes out. It also ensures that the drill must be unplugged whenever you adjust the bit.

Predrilling (Make room for the screw!)

In today's world, a screw pistol, or a driver-bit drill, is sometimes used to drive screws, making pre-drilling redundant.

We highly advocate, though, that learning to drive screws by hand is a fundamental ability that should be learned by all carpenters, and it is an individual endeavor that does not involve adult supervision.

It is hard work to push a screw into two pieces of wood with a screwdriver, though.

Using it can also contribute to damaged or misdirected screws and a frustrating finish to the job without first pre-drilling space for the screw to move through. So, we have called for pre-drilling in virtually every case in this book that requires r using screws.

Chapter 8
Measurement

It may take a while to get to the stage for young carpenters to trust their measuring and labeling skills. A necessity for happy building is a skill with the calculation of tools. But only time and experience will fulfill this contented condition. Any simple instruments for measuring are mentioned in this section and how to manage and use them to the maximum effect.

The Tape and Ruler, Measurement Apparatus

The ruler is the easiest of the measurement instruments and is, therefore, a convenient straight surface for drawing lines. The extendable metal-bladed tape measure is most carpenters' favorite measurement instrument. It is also used to calculate long lengths, not as a straight surface for drawing lines. One point to remember about the tape measure is that the hooked end on the tape often feels loose. This action makes up for the width of the end of the tape by comparing inside and outside.

Three Square

The three square is an outstanding instrument. Not only you can use it to calculate short lengths or square a line (draw a line to one side of a board at a 90-degree angle), but you can also use it to draw lines at an angle.

The Speed Square renders it easier to create a straight line since it has a lip or flanged hand, which is tightly resting on a board's edge. A tape measure is needed to map lengths on a long surface, but the Pace Square is the instrument of preference when it's time to create an angled or a straight-line pad for certain points.

Similar to Speed Square, the combination square can be used for several of the same jobs. The fundamental distinction is that there are dimensions marked on his ruler, and the ruler is movable. You may reposition it to easily measure some length from the side of a board by easing a knob. The square often has a level, which can be really helpful at times.' A steel framing square is an important tool for difficult tasks such as building rafters and stairs in the hands of a skilled carpenter. However, children are more inclined to value the framing square as a right-angled ruler. The framing square is the best instrument for calculating "over and in." since i measurements

are marked on all of its four long sides. You can calculate 12 inches from the edge of a frame, square a line to label the range, and find a point 4 inches from the end of that line - all in a single move '

The long side of A framing square' measures around 24 inches and is called the blade or the body. The instrument is 16 inches long on the shorter hand and is named the toggle. The blade is 2 inches in width while the tongue is 1 1/ inches in width; these sizes refer to rough-sawn and dressed wood.

Line Squaring

Squaring a line specifically indicates drawing a line perpendicular to a straight edge (at a 90-degree angle). You will square lines over a board in most situations.

To square, a line, keep one edge of your square (speed square flanged side, combination square handle, or framing square body) to the edge of your board. Slide the square until it hits the spot where you want the line to start and draw a line across the board there, holding the pencil stable against the straight side of the square, the top corner (where the two edges of the square intersect at a right angle).

Direct measurement

One of the easiest methods (without a ton of tools) to tackle every measuring job is to put the piece you need to carve in the place that it needs to match and directly marking the appropriate length on it. You would not have to apply or deduct percentages or fractions of inches to scare you! If you are constructing a project and one of the parts needs to fit in a specific location, consider marking it off explicitly instead of depending on the calculated measurements. You would be walking in the footsteps of experienced carpenters such as cabinetmakers and stair builders, who, by drawing lines on aboard length to signify the location of door edges, windowsills, and electrical outlets, establish their own "ruler" of a space. If you need several parts of one pan, cutting one and having it as a guide to cut the others can be easier than measuring and labeling each one.

The Paper ruler

The challenge with the measurement system we inherited from English is how difficult it is to apply. Its fundamental principle is clear, though. A single measure (the inch), which is derived from the size of three barely grains placed end to end, is split in half and then literally split over and over again before we enter the 32nds of an inch indicated on most rulers.

To understand the perplexing profusion of marks on a ruler, it will be a good approach for aspiring carpenters is to create their own. They 'will make a helpful fraction comparison in the process.

Get a sheet of paper that is unlined (approximately 8 by 11 inches). Fold the sheet lengthwise in two. Draw a line down half the length of this fold and mark it 1/2. Both sides of this fold constitute half of the total paper length (from the fold to the sheet's edge).

Fold in one of the outside edges such that it aligns with the 1/2 point in the middle of the page and creases it back. Open the fold, trace about a quarter of the length of the fold, and label 1/4. Duplicate this procedure on the opposite side of the sheet. Keep dividing the sheet by half, moving from the outer edges into the last fraction you have labeled. The outcome is a double-ended "ruler," which can calculate fractions on a sheet of paper for household items. You'll have to put the fractions together to calculate the length of an item

that is more than half the length of a page to achieve the right measurement. It may be a little frustrating at first, but it's a great exercise for calculating.

Chapter 9

Projects

Few activities are as enjoyable and exciting but also satisfying as completing a project with your children. They get the pleasure of engaging their imaginations and utilizing resources as adults.

Parents get the joy of investing some time doing something meaningful for the young kids, educating and making something over a period that the family will appreciate.

These activities are all child-friendly. They may present some challenges. You could also produce a progression of tasks such that you can pass from one project to the next with growing complexity if your children enjoy working with their hands. Some of them are very basic and only feature wood, glue, and paint. Some require electrical instruments. That also implies they need a lot of adult guidance as well.

The best thing is that children will center their imagination because there are no incorrect answers at their simplest.

In contexts of supplies and fasteners, each one has its own particular requirements. How-to guides and images of raw materials and what the final product might appear like are also provided.

Select the best one for your children to transform a special rainy day into a special day.

Holey Name

Here's the skill builder, which will offer lots of drilling practice. Not just, you're going to end up in lights with your name (sunlight that is).Set up two or three drills with the multiple bits (of several sizes, if you have them); this way, you can only change tools whenever you choose to create a different-sized hole instead of wasting your time swapping bits.

Tools and materials:

- Tools
- Pencil
- Protective Glasses
- Cordless or electric drill (s)
- Drill bit of 1/2-inch
- Drill bit of 1/4inch
- Drill bit of 1/8-inch
- Clamps
- Materials
- Small ½-inch Luaun or birch plywood
- Wood scrap (plank or plywood)

- Ribbon, Rope, or Braided Yarn

Instructions

1. Write your name on the plywood board with a pencil. Block letters will make up for the clearest job, but try a fancy cursive if you like to go for a greater challenge.

2. Put marks on your name where you want the holes to to be drilled.

3. Use a measurement instrument to mark drilling spots at frequent intervals if you desire the holes to be equally distributed. To decide whether they are too near or far removed from each other, take a glance at the marks. Note, the marks all together should be identifiable as your name!

4. Under the ply board with your name, put a piece of wood scrap, and firmly clamp all parts to your worktop. Put your safety eyewear on and get to work on all the lines you have drawn for drilling holes. Choose the same bit or combine the bit sizes for all of them. Just make sure to drill into your board any hole straight through.

Let it shine

1. Drill a hole in both upper corners of the board to create a convenient hanging mechanism. Pull the cord's length, string, or

threaded yam through the holes and attach the ends together to form

a circle. Display your name board in the window. When the sun is up,

the light will shine across the letters of your name.

String Art sculpture

This project offers woodworkers lots of exercise hammering, measuring - and cutting, and some value stringing time, also! A wonderful work of sculpture will come from meticulous measuring and preparation, but also rendered by free-form shaping, unplanned

securing, and wild abandonment, can emerge an interesting item.

Tools and materials:

- Tools
- Handsaw
- Hammer
- Your preferred instruments for measurement
- Pencil
- Material
- Yarn or string
- Scraps of Wood
- Nails (shingle nails or 4d galvanized box nails)
- Fasteners

Instructions

1. Pick a slab of wood which is appealing to you. Make it on any size, but it will give better results when it' is at least 14 inches in length. Cutting it with a handsaw if you like your piece to be of a

special size or form will give it a unique look. For a 3D String Art design, you may also nail together one or two bits of wood.

Measurement

2. If you want to create a completely free-form path it is your choice. Otherwise, trace on the wood board a line (or lines) to mark the nails' possible location, using a pencil and any measurement toolsquare or a ruler for straight lines or a compass for circles.

3. On the line or lines, you have just drawn, Measure and label the precise positions at even intervals where you want your nails to be.

Straight-Line

4. Using the ruler or measurement tape, mark every 1/2 or 1 inch to space nails equally on a straight line,

Circles

5. Set the compass in a way that its two legs are 1/2 to 1 inch apart to space the nails evenly along a circle. On the circle line, position the compass point. Spin the compass's pencil-holding leg around.

6. When it crosses the line of the circle, make a marking at that point. Move the compass's pointed end to the marking you have recently made and make another marking where the pen now cuts the circle's line. Do this process all-round the circle all the way. If the last markings are not properly spaced, try adjusting them by

the eye.

Hammer time!

7. Insert nails where you have labeled or if you are making a freeform piece, anywhere you desire. Yeah, wherever you like it. Only

push the nails in the board until they are securely set; don't hammer them in the board all the way. Make sure the nail tops are just at the equal height when you're finished.

Stringing

8. The finale is here! Tie the string securely, near to the head, on the first nail. If it is circle stringing, begin with any nail. Begin with a nail at the end of the line if you are stringing a line. If you work on an abstract piece, just string away. If you work on asymmetrical style, follow a string pattern, like the Sunshine, Sunset, Double Bridge, or Arrow (see the instructions below). Whichever design you pick, remember to keep the string tight while you work.

9. When you're finished then, tie the string tightly to the last nail, and clip with scissors the ends of the thread.

Sunshine (circle nails):

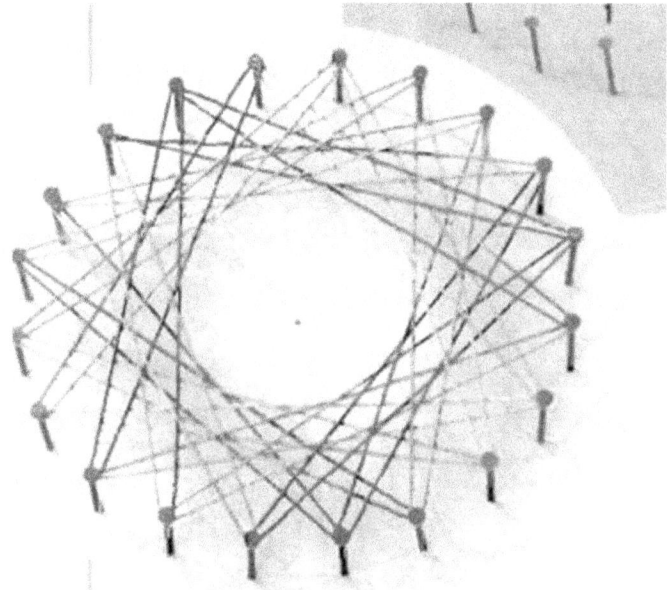

Attach the cord to any of the nail. Pull the cord toward the right of the beginning nail, and attach to the 7th nail. When the cord is wound around the nail, take it down to the nail just right to your starting nail.

Wind the cord on the nail and again take it to the 7th nail to the right.

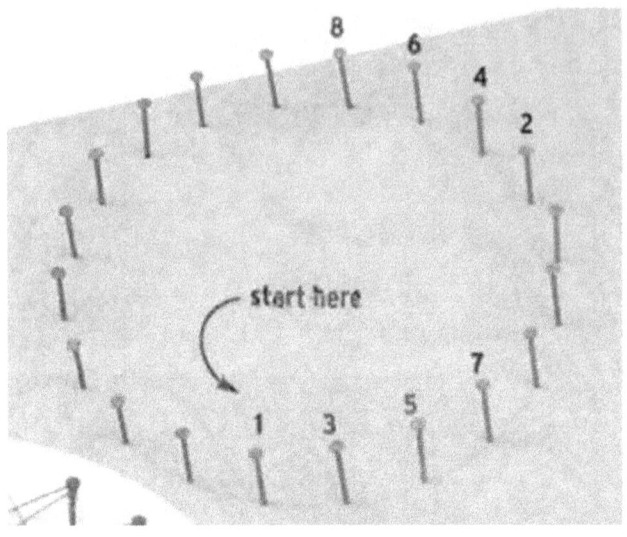

Once more, loop the cord around the nail thoroughly and then take the cord back to the nail to rightwards of the previous stringed nail. Proceed through the whole circle this way - seven onward, six backward. (Doesn't need to be 7; you can make this pattern skipping onward any figure of nails you select Just choose a number and stay with it.)

Sunset

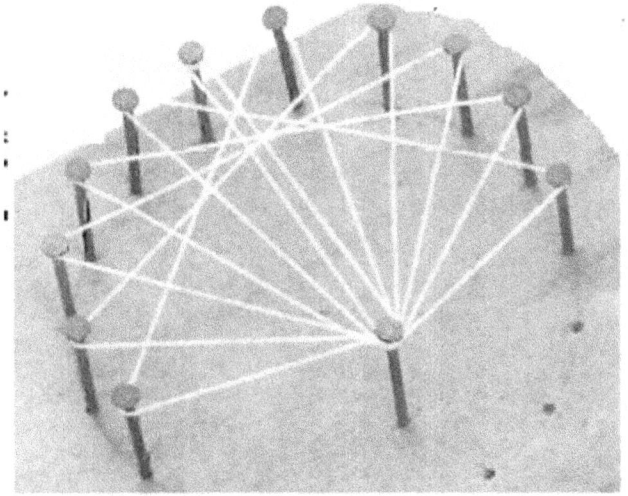

Wrap the thread to a single nail. (A semi - circle of pins facing a single pin). Take the thread to semicircle's leftmost nail. Wrap it round this nail once, and then put it to the sixth nail to its right side. Wrap this nail around it, then bring the string down to the single nail. Then bring the string and loop around the single nail and take it to the semi circle's second nail. Loop it around the nail once, then drag it to the right of the nail with six nails. Loop this nail through it and return to the Single Nail. Keep going in this manner, making the way from six nails out from each of the nail in the half circle to its neighbor and then return to the lone single nail until each nail has been stringed once. In the end, tie your cord in the lone single nail, and you 'are done.'

The Arrow

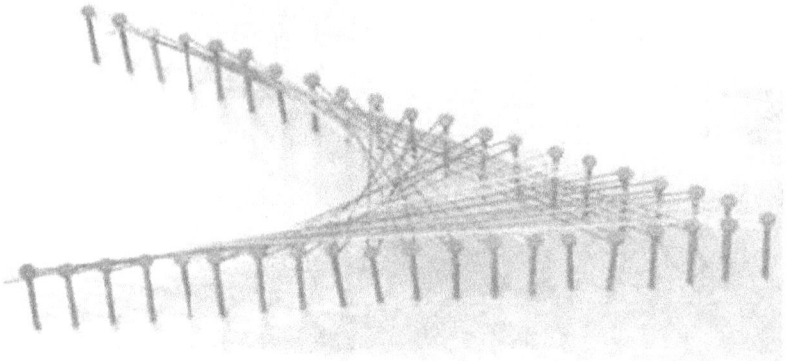

Shit the board such that it is upside down with the V. On the line at right side, connect the cord to the last nail. From the V shape point, draw the cord toward the nail. If you tie the string around this nail all the way round, then take it down to the next-to-last pin on the righthand side. Tie the string round this nail fully, then pull it to the left side line of the first nail on the Vpoint. Pull the string round this nail fully around and take it back two points away from the beginning nail to the nail. Repeat this way, then pass the string down both lines along with one pin at a time.

Double Bridge (3D art)

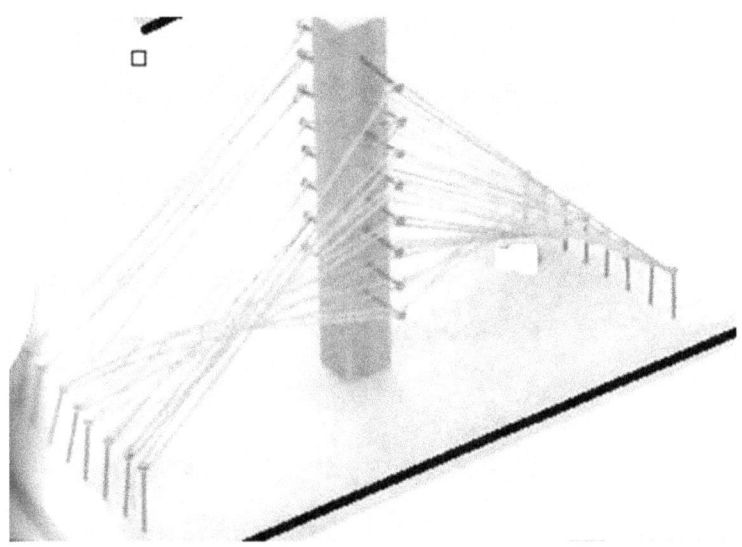

Connect your string to one of the vertical rows of nails at the top to one of the nails on horizontal rows, pull the thread to the last nail on the same side of the frame. Draw the string round this nail, then move it from the top of the vertical line to the second nail. From there, go to the horizontal second nail, backwards to the third vertical nail, and so forth, till all the nails on those horizontal and vertical rows have been wound around the string by you. When you come to the edge of the horizontal row, pull the string from the nail at the edge of that line to the top most nail on the outside vertical row ark back down the nails again on that horizontal row (now each one will have a string around it) before you get to the end.

Now take the string on the first vertical row to the topmost t nail.

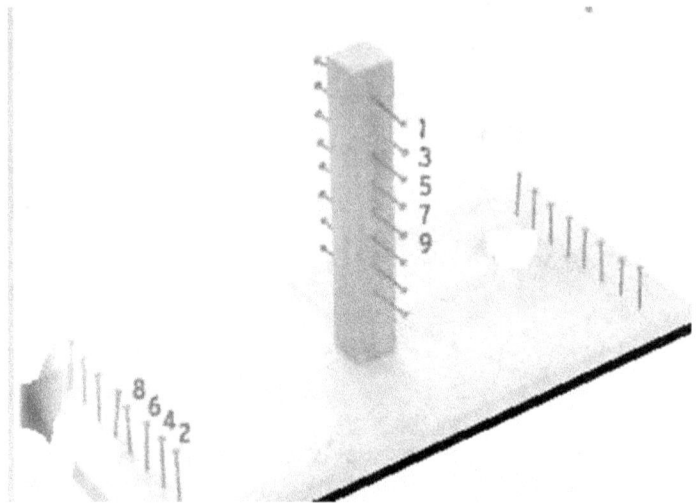

Repeat the procedure until you have finished down the other horizontal row. And you are done.

Bird Houses

Without birdhouses, no collection of woodworking projects for kids will be complete. It is a nice moderate difficulty project created at some stage by just about any child. They help our fine feathered friends with living space and encourage your children to take more complicated efforts to work with wood and equipment.

Here is an easy design to make a birdhouse of your own. For children with adult support, it is a wonderful project.

So, assemble a few materials and get to work.

Tools and materials:

- Small nails or brads 1" long for assembly
- Hammer
- Saw of your choice
- Measuring tape
- 1 rod– 3/8" dowel 8" in length
- 1 board of pine – 1 X 6 cut into
- 2 squares of - 5 1/2-inch X 5 1/2 inch (you can use other types of
- wood, i.e., cedar)
- 1 Fir plywood – 3/16 " cut into
- 1 board of- 6" X 8 inch and 5 rectangles of –13/16" X 8 inch
- 1 – 4" diameter perforated PVC pipe cut 5 inches long
- 2 – #212 eye hooks

- 12 inches wire or small chain for hanging

Instructions

1. Size the panels and cut them.

You will get a 1 –3/8″ dowel rod 8″ long, 5″ length of 4″ PVC pipe, 5

roof pieces of 13/16″ X 8-piece, 1 piece 6 X 8″ roof piece, and 2 pieces pine squares of 5 1/2″.

2. Drill holes of 3/8" in the particular way on the 5 ½" squares.

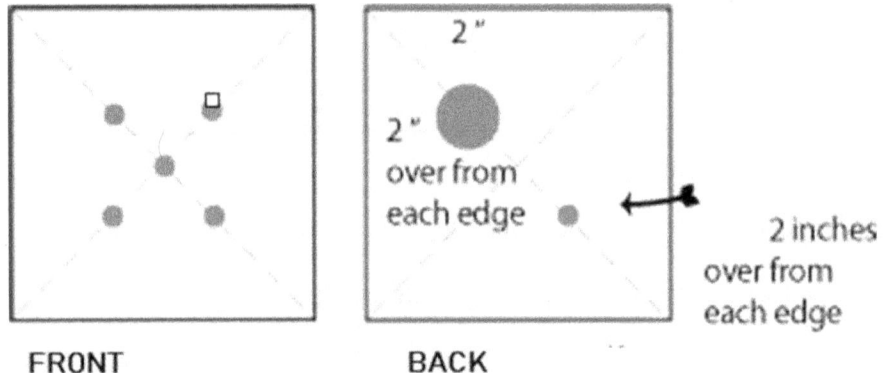

Using

a 1 1/4-inch spade drill bit for the bigger hole.

3. Smooth the edges of all the pieces by sanding.

4. Now it's hammer using time! Nail the squares of 5 ½" leveled

With the sides of the 5 13/16" by 8" roof piece. The pre-drilled holes

For nails make it simpler for kids to hammer the nails in.

5. Overlap another roof piece (6" by 8 ") and nail it to the top flanks of the 5 ½" square.

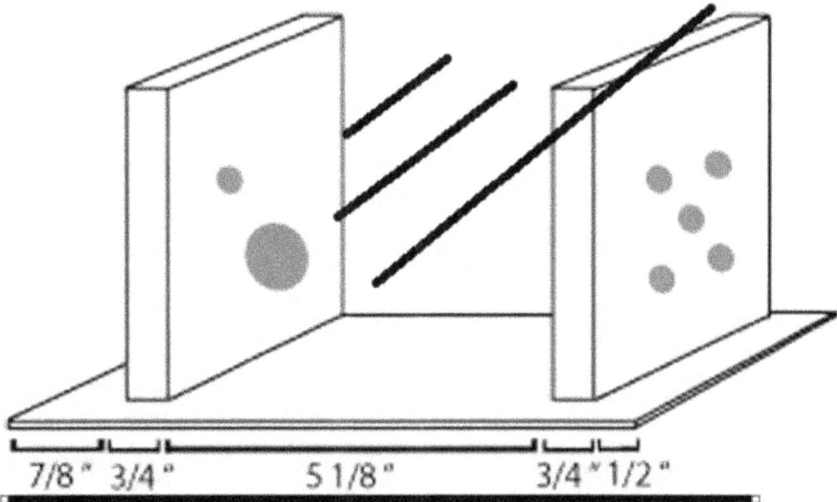

6. Put the PVC pipe on the underside the roof and keep it in place by pushing in the dowel rod over the holes under the bottom. The dowel will fit tightly securing the pipe. You can also sand it lightly if desired.

Birds enjoy getting neat homes! The tidy thing about this wooden birdhouse is that to have an airflow, the PVC piping is holed and can quickly be detached for cleaning. For each side, screw on the eye hooks to the roof. Then tie the eye hooks to the chain. Completed!

Toothbrush Holders

It's cool for them to see their creativity come to life. I admire how the kids choose what ways they can be. And they were enthusiastic about cleaning their teeth finally!

Tools and materials:

- Safety glasses
- Pencil
- Saw of your choice
- Drill
- 1" Forstner bit
- Sandpaper
- Materials
- 2x6 wood scrap

Instructions

1. Grab a 2x6 scrap and get your child to draw whatever form they want.

Printable models can be found, but I think it's more enjoyable for kids

to be creatively open.

2. Cut the form out of it!

You would have to do this procedure with them, based on how old your child is. A band saw, jigsaw, or scroll saw may be used. In reality, a scroll saw is a perfect first power tool to introduce to children.

3. Drill a hole on the side of the piece for the toothbrush!

To drill this out, use a 1" Forstner bit. Children want to use the drill, make it enjoyable and safe for them. Make sure to wear safety glasses,

Just ensure it's all clamped up pretty tight.

4. Sand and paint, it! Both are activities which children love to do!

And they are done!

Banana Holder

Tools and materials

- Compass
- Pencil
- Ruler
- Plain saw
- Drill
- 3/4" plywood sheet or any wood scrap
- 3/4" dowel (for holder)
- 3/8" dowel (for hook)
- Glue
- Paints

Instructions

1. Using a compass, measure to 4-1/2" and make a 9" loop.

It will be the basis of the banana holder, and you can use whatever material you want!

We used a sheet of 3/4" plywood, while it would be cool if you could stick any scraps together to make this happen!

2. Make the base out of the circle!

The base does not at all have to be a circle. You can create it in whatever form you choose.

3. Cut a 3/4" dowel to 12" in length for the stand. Hand tools are a perfect way to get the kids interested in the workshop; they love to use saws like this!

4. Cut the 3/8" dowel to about 4" to make the hook.

5. To place the 3/8" dowel hook, drill a hole, at an angle, into the stand.

This position or angle doesn't need to be accurate; just eyeball it!

6. To insert the 3/4" dowel stand onto the base, drill a 3/4" hole in the

base. Do not drill the whole way in.

Again, this doesn't need to be in a particular spot; it should be a side of the circle, not in the center.

7. Glue the dowels on the base. Gluing is an activity that children would love to do!

Sand it, and it's done!

Lego Coat Hanger

The best addition to a kid's space or mudroom is this Lego coat hanger. The best thing is building it is simple. AND boys love it

Tools and materials

- Drill kit 18v
- 10 inches. sliding compound miter saw
- Mailer brad
- 2x4, wooden dowel,
- Coat hooks,
- Nail filler,
- Acrylic paint,
- D-rings,
- Wood glue,
- Foam brushes,
- Polyacrylic paint

Instructions

1. First, cut the 2 & 4 down to the dimensions you like. The one created HERE has a length of 36 inches, and a miter saw is used for cutting. To sand, use a sander to make it smooth. Cut the dowel rod into half inch sized pieces. Sand the ends when, once you've cut them, they would most definitely be a little splintery or

rough.

2. To fashion the Lego look following pattern was used: short Lego (with 4 dowel pieces), coat hook, long Lego (with 6 dowel pieces), coat hook, short Lego, hook, long Lego, hook, and short Lego. At this stage, there is not much calculation; just spread the dowel parts in the place where you need them (leave the spots for "hook" unmarked at first, then eyeball everything to ensure that all is even.

3. Second, on the dowel pieces' backs, dot a bit of wood glue and hammer them with the brad nailer in place. Ensure that the brad nails sink into the wood enough that you can cover them

4. After the nail hole filling had dried, its painting time, it is the most exciting aspect of the kids' entire project! You need clean, crisp lines, so divide the Legos using painter's tape, and paint one color at a time, allowed it to dry, then reapply the tape next to the one you have already painted to paint the "Lego." To reach through all of the nooks and corners, use a combination of the foam brush and a little artist's paintbrush. Two coats of paint should be used to give a good finished look; With Minwax Polyacrylic, seal the entire thing.

5. Place the hooks where you need them. Use a pencil to map the holes, then drill small pilot holes. Screw the hooks on and then

attach the D-Rings to the back to mount it on the wall.

Wooden Box Planter

To sit on top of the railing, bring elegance to your deck by constructing planter boxes. For an inexperienced woodworker, this is a perfect project. It can be made according to any size you desire.

Tools and materials

- Screwdriver
- Saw
- Tape measure
- Drills
- Screws (galvanized)
- Brackets mounting
- Boards
- Cleats of Wood

- Screen

Instructions

1. Cut and assemble the boards

Determine the planter box's size. Using pressure-treated wood is best. The side pieces and the end pieces can be cut to the size you choose. Now fasten them using galvanized screws together.

Measure the inside length and width of the box. Cut a panel to fit the

bottom and nail the bottom with galvanized screws on the edges.

2. Fixing the cleat to the wooden box

Add the cleats and drill holes for drainage. Attach the cleats to the underside of the box. It will offer you a good profile and protect the railing from being damaged over time.

Drill the bottom of the box for three or four drainage holes.

3. Insert a Liner

Cut a Liner and Insert it

Cut a vinyl or nylon screen panel to fit into the box's rim. The screen can help to keep the gravel and the soil in the box.

4. Attaching to a Deck

You should directly screw the box onto the railing of your deck. A store-bought bracket device that connects to the side of the railing is another alternative to use.

X-Shaped Minimal Coaster Set

Coasters are important to protect tabletop surfaces, but they are also clunky and dull, so why not build something that not only rocks your drink but is also visually interesting? The balsa pre-cut strips, a softwood that prevents the need for a saw, can be used to create this graphic 'X' type DIY coasters. Create a collection for yourself this weekend, and add a sculptural set that functions overtime as contemporary art for those mundane coasters! (Heavy-duty scissors are good enough for the job!)

Tools and materials

- 1/4" Thick balsa wood strips are generally available in a range of
- wood strip lengths at the hardware store.

- Glue for All-Purpose
- Black paint spray
- Ruler or T Square
- Sandpaper
- Scissors
- Pencil

Instructions

1. Using a powerful heavy-duty scissor, cut 2 strips of balsa wood about 4″ long each. Label the center of each strip using a straight edge.

2. Place in the middle of one strip a dot of all-purpose glue and place the other strip on top of it, matching the central mark from step one and creating an "X" pattern. Allow it to dry out.

3. "Place next to one "leg" of the "X" yet another 1/4" strip and mark the length to cut. At this mark, cut the strip.

4. Attach the strip you cut to the leg of the 'X' with glue. Tightly press together and clean out the extra glue.

5. Repeat steps 3 & 4 until the "X" is flat on both sides.

6. To build a set of 4 coasters, replicate the above steps three more times. Sand the rough edges off.

7. Color coasters with black paint spray. 2 coats for either side of it. Please enable it to completely dry.

DIY Children's Wooden Texture Stamps

Wooden stamps Creativity is a wonderful experience. Inspire yourself by learning how to apply a texture to the wood, and you will be motivated to use similar techniques to create these charming texture stamps of DIY wood. Lately, this has become more popular.

Tools and materials

- A thick branch
- A SMALL saw (pocket-sized)
- Sand Paper
- Hammer
- Nails
- A Screw
- A Nut
- A chisel (the tool is not a chisel in the image, but it's similar)

Instructions

1. Saw a thick branch into parts 12 cm apart.

2. Use sandpaper to tidy and smooth the branch's top, bottom, and sides.

3 Grab a hammer and one of your tools. At first, let's use a nut. Position the nut on the upper, smooth side of the wood, and then strike it hard with a hammer or mallet. The deeper the imprint in

the wood, the higher the result of subsequent stamping. Space out

the nut creases on the wooden top to create a template.

Wood Nature

Crafts

4. Perform this technique for all the stamps, excluding the screw. Position the screw on its side and hammer its t side into the wood. You can flip over the branch stump to construct another pattern on the other side or use them as singular stamps,

5. When you're done, give a light sanding to the top.

6. Time for painting and fun!

We noticed that when a towel was put under the paper, the wooden stamps came out with a stronger print.

Children's First Tool Kit Box

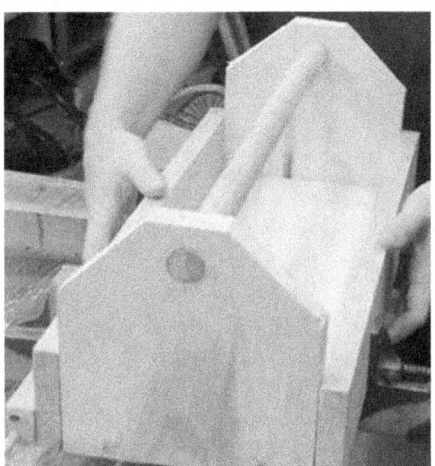

This Tool Kit is a perfect first-time venture as you will learn how to use a saw, a brace, a hand plane, and a brace & bit, and even dowel carpentry. Most kids will have to do this project with a parent's little support and guidance and then have the pleasure of creating the first tool they will use for years to come.

- Tools and materials
- Hand Plane
- Hand Saw
- Brace -
- Collection of Bits
- Cutting saw flush
- Clamps

- V-tool Carving Chisel
- The Supplies
- Adhesive
- Dowel 3/8"
- 1" dowel
- Oak 1X4
- Oak 1X8

Instructions

1. Size Cut

Usually, a western panel saw is used for crosscutting the log, but the sharper blade of a Japanese pull saw is simpler for children. Launch the hack, then keep your hands over there to teach them how to use the saw, and in a few minutes, they will be off to the timber cutting races.

The same is applies to the angles on the two end parts. Only place them at 45 degrees in a vice, then let them cut them off.

2. Drill the Hole for the Handel

For all of the end pieces cut off, you should clamp them together and

cut out the 1" space for the handle with a drill. It's better to clamp them together so that the holes match up in the future.

It is also a perfect way to learn how a brace functions. Let the children keep it in position as the handle is cranked.

3. Bottom and Ends Bind

It is better to drill the pin holes through the ends and down the bottom before glue-up. This step helps glue-up even easier, although it can also be achieved after glue-up.

Kids should now be familiar with the brace, and they can drill the smaller 3/8" hole independently.

Begin by drilling 3 holes along the end caps' rim. Then transfer the markings of the holes to the ends of the bottom piece. Last, cut the bottom holes. You're ready to glue it together now.

4. Key Assembly of Glue Up

Let the kids feel the joy of placing the glue in and putting it in place to clamp. Make sure you have the handle in position before you clamp it up.

5. Set up Dowels

Now that the adhesive has been set up, we can push in the dowels,

then cut them flat with a flush-cut saw. As this is what helps hold the

entire thing together, make sure you use sufficient glue.

It is a perfect way to teach how a mallet should be kept and how a flush-cut saw functions.

6. The side panels are to be connected

For side panels, it's pretty simple to set up and tighten them up. The glue can conveniently hold them together with the long grain before you place the dowels in.

Using the brace and bit again after glue-up, to drill seven holes each side. Two will go through each of the end caps, and three will go in the bottom. You will then replicate the last stage and push in dowels and cut them off flush.

7. Carve and Smooth

This step is the best chance to practice how to use a hand plane to tidy out the joints by smoothing out the dowels.

8. FINISHING it!!!!

Applying the finish is the last step. After applying on 3 coats, we declared it done.

Tree DIY Swing

In the process of upgrading a backyard play space. The broken swings can be made easily. Creating your own swings is surprisingly simple, and it doesn't take very long. When I told Mike what I had in mind, he instantly blew off two swings – slowed down only by preventing his wife from taking pictures of him.

Tools and materials

- Wood (use pine wood)
- Rope (use a 3/" nylon rope – ensure working load level is high
- enough for anybody who is going to use the swing)
- Saw
- Drill's
- Roader/Sand Paper

Instructions

1. Assess the length you intend your swing to be, then cut the length of the board.

2. Use the sandpaper or a router to round the corners of the cut board. Sand any hard spots around the swing.

3. Assess and mark the openings that your rope will pass through. Drill holes, make sure you use a drill bit that's as wide as the string you're using.

4. To fasten the rope: keep the rope as one long length, slip one end

of the rope into a hole beginning at the top of the swing. Pull the rope around the base of the swing and up the next hole. String up a knot. Take the remainder of the rope and loop it into the gaps on the other side, beginning at the top of the swing and moving it up and down. Tie the other knot. Now the rope on the swing should be a huge loop; locate the middle of the rope and cut it off such that the rope is now divided.

5. To guarantee that the rope's cut ends are not unraveled/frayed, you may melt the ends with a lighter or tie them with twine. Hang out on the tree branch and make sure both knots are quite tight.

Folding Dollhouse

There are several choices for this idea. You can build it on any size to meet your particular requirements, and you should incorporate as little or as much decoration as you choose! Some of the supplies were not used and ended up not used in this project but addition of shingles, or painted bricks could be something I'll incorporate if I build more of these fold-away houses for my dolls one day.

Tools and materials

- Miter scissors or sharp cutters
- Efficiency drill
- Jigsaw
- T square
- (optional) brushes or sponges

Material:

- 1/2" of plywood (1/4 of whole sheet)
- Hinges to be used for the front door and the walls (the size varies
- on the dimension, but you will need to buy short screws so that
- they don't poke through the plywood).
- The trim pieces of basswood
- Sandpaper (use 400 grit, 120 grit, and 80 grit.)

- Glue of wood
- Pencil
- Prime + paint
- Painter's masking tape (optional)

Instructions

1. Cut the plywood to the proportions you like for dollhouse walls to be. We made walls of 22"by16" for a 7" doll. Then mark where you would like your doors, windows, and rooflines to be, using a square or T-square.

2. Using a jigsaw, remove out the forms you traced in first step.

A new portion of wood piece for the front door will also need to be cut. Make it narrower than the gap, so the hinges and swings would make it properly fit than you think.

3. Smooth off all the rough ends with a block covered in sandpaper of 80 grit. Once you've smooth off the jigsaw cut pieces' rough edges, go over with sandpaper of 120 grit to keep everything clean and smooth.

4. Cut parts of your basswood trims to serve as trim all around the doors, windows, and floors. Fix each piece to the door walls and using wood adhesive, then "lock" the parts in position with the masking tape till the glue has been dried.

You could color the trim individually and stick it on after coloring the walls, and you can also paint with spray the entire thing, trim and everything, then fill it in with color. If your stencil on some template, adding the trims after painting will be wise.

At this stage, you may opt to keep your wood unpainted and normal. Whether that's what you'd want.

If you're going to keep the walls and doors unpainted, be sure to seal it all with a couple of polyurethane coats. Light sanding with sandpaper of 400 grit on the first coat guarantees that the end results are clean and silky.

5. Prime the door and the walls and also paint them. Using sandpaper of 400 grit after a coat of primer to make the exterior clean. Then switch on to the final colors of the canvas.

You can wallpaper the inside walls with small flower wallpaper, but the wallpaper will end peeling up with long usages and wear and tears, leave it as non-destructible as possible.

6. To link the walls, add the hinges. Make sure you stagger the hinges up one side or down the other side of the center frame, or else your bolts on either side of the hinges will strike one another and cause you a load of grief.

Family Name from a Pallet

Don't you love all the fun stuff you see on Pinterest that can be made from a pallet? Name signs are a fad these days. You can purchase the signs and get your family's name placed on them, but that can get pricey. So, we got imaginative and came up with a really awesome family sign from the Pallet!

Tools and materials

- A palette
- Your name in vinyl (you can make one by using a circuit machine
- or a silhouette cameo machine)
- Small nails
- Hanger to hang it on a photo wire
- A saw to cut the pallet wood

Instructions

In only a few quick steps, you can create this sign.

1. Take the Pallet apart. It's a lot simpler than you expect.

2. If you need to, cut it according to the size you desire and determine how many planks of wood you need.

3. Break up another strip of the Pallet to serve as a support on the rear. On the back, nail this to attach all the pieces of wood. We are not using glue, as we don't want it to appear perfect.

Remember, it's a pallet; it should appear uneven and unfinished, giving it a rustic style.

4. Now add the hanger to the back.

5. Finish it off with vinyl

6. You just need to hang it now that it is done. If you want it to last longer, try adding a seal on vinyl and wood to prevent any peeling.

Simple Homemade Candy Dispenser

It is a candy dispenser that is really simple to create. It's very good to do this for children from 6 to 12 years of age to introduce woodworking. They're trying to make their first Candy Dispenser unit!

Tools and materials

- 2" by 6" board, 24" long
- Size the boards:
- 2 boards of 1 1/2" by 5 1/2" by 5 1/2" (for base and top)

- 2 boards of 1 1/2" by 1 3/4" by 5 1/2" (for the sides)
- 1 board of 1" by 1 7/8" by 11" (for the slide)
- Pencil
- Pocketknife
- Wood glue
- Tape measure
- Sandpaper
- 1 peg or dowel 4" long, with a dia of around 1/4"
- 1 peg or dowel, 2" long with a dia of around 1/4"
- Mason jar
- Beans or gumballs or any round candy
- Ripsaw
- Crosscut saw
- Drill
- Spade bit of 7/8"
- Drill bit, 2 1/2" holes (for pre-drilling)
- Bit of countersink (so screws are driven flat)
- Screwdrivers
- Wood screws, 2 ½" long, 12 pcs.
- Drill bit, small (for pre-drilling of container ring brad holes)

- Flat-head brads, 4pcs. (For nailing the container ring at the top of
- the dispenser).

Instructions

1. Cut to a scale of all the panels and sand smoothly.

2. Glue the foundation to the sides and screw it on.

3. Mark an X on the top of the board from corner to corner.

4. Drill a hole of 7/8″ through the middle of the board's top.

5. Glue the top panel on the sides and foundation and screw it. Sand the slider until the in the middle square hole of the dispenser; it slides effortlessly.

6. Drill a 3/4″ opening on the front of the slider. It will make a hole for

the dowel or the 4″ peg. Drill 1/2″ of a cavity from the other side of the slider. This one is for a dowel or peg of 2". Glue the 4" dowel or peg onto the slider in the front hole.

7. Move the slider into position until at the 4" peg it stops. Make a circle on the slide from the 7/8″ opening of the board on top.

8. Drill a hole of 7/8″ in the slider which is 3/8″ deep

9. With a pocketknife bevel the slider hole of 7/8". and then sand it smooth,

10. Drill the container ring and nail it to the top panel.

11. Push the slider to the correct spot. If the slider is moved in completely, the hole of the slider and the hole on the top must match up. On the back of the slider, glue the 2" dowel or peg.

12. Fill the candy jar, screw it into the attached lid, and the dispenser is ready.

Simple Hinged Box

We are going to use a technique for creating a little box with wood hinges that are integrated. You may as well make this one inside the dining room, as this would not need any elaborate gear and can be achieved quite easily. The corner seams are basic lap joints.

Tools and Materials

- Clamps (small)
- Ruler or Tape Measuring
- One nail of 2 inches length, around.
- Miter and saw set, or table saw.
- Drill
- Sand Paper
- Two bits of different sizes (one wider and one smaller than the
- required screw).
- Glue for Wood (in this project, for the hinge parts "gorilla glue" Is
- recommended)
- Wood - 1 -4-foot- 1 by 44 (or the remains of the wood from the
- earlier work)
- A small spare bit of scrap wood.

Instructions

Here we dive into the dangerous realm of electrical instruments, SO BE ALERT. Some of the stages here will require drilling on small pieces of wood. Here you should keep the parts against a wood scrap, and the wood scrap must be on a table or board. Never support the parts on yourself while drilling.

Pick the board and size it into pieces below:

For the Box

- 3 Pieces- of 6 inches. Each
- 2 Pieces of- 4 & 1/4 inch each
- 1 Piece of- 7 & 1/2 inches.
- For the Hinge (now for the complicated ones)
- 2 Blocks of ¾" x ¾".
- 1 Block of 3" x ¾". One end rounded with a sandpaper or a sander.

A simple structure of boxes:

1. Begin with 2 of the six-inch pieces. Attach them together to make an 'L' shape with glue, make sure you properly line up the corners.

2. Clamp them and let it dry for one hour.

3. Remove the box from the clamps and glue the two final pieces together.

4. Use two clamp methods to lock the ends in position. Let them dry

for at least one hour.

5. Glue the last six-inch piece after un-clamping the piece, ensuring all of the edges that meet are glued.

6. clamps the entire thing again, making certain it does not move. Overnight, let dry.

Construction of the Top and Hinge:

Use Gorilla glue for the hinges parts will be my best advice. It's just tougher.

1. With the bigger of the two drill bits, take the round ended 3-inch by

3/4-inch block and the 3/4-inch square blocks and make a hole through the middle with a drill.

2. Get the last square block of ¾"and drill with the small bit through the middle

Now via one square block and the 3-inch block, you should be able to move the screw and then secure it into the last wood block (with the small hole). It is critical to pre-drill the given spaces in this way. If you don't, the wood can break. I'm guaranteeing it.

3. See if the measure suits the given screw by moving it into the large-hole ¾" block, then the 3" block, and through the small-hole ¾" block, don't tighten anything too hard. All pieces need to spin freely also. As far as it's all decent looking, carry on. Drill the holes

in with a little bigger bit.

Put aside the assembled parts.

4. Position the 7 ½ inch piece on upper part of the completed box

So that you get a flat surface to assemble the Hinge.

5. Locate and indicate the center of the back upright portion. It is expected to be 3 inches.

6. Attach the two blocks with glue in position. Glue the blocks' bottoms ONLY. You must do all you can to hold the adhesive off the 3" block and also the 7 ½" cover.

7. Put a pair of smaller clamps in position and tighten. Take off the screw, the 3" block, and the top piece carefully when it is set. To prevent the squeezed-out adhesive from holding together pieces that don't fit together.

8. Later, when the adhesive has been left for a period of time and no further damp spots are seen, put back the 3" block and cover, keeping the small clamps in position.

9. Making sure the top of the box is straight, glue the 3-inch block on it. Be sure to keep the adhesive away from the side of the back. We do not want to squeeze it all out to seal the back of the top.

10. Let all of this dry for a night.

Take the clamps off from this stuff and admire them. The Hinge ought to operate reasonably smoothly. It's not unusual to get a bit of a sloppy finish. Using two hinges will be ideal,

If you try sanding the box, consider disassembling the top of the box prior to testing it out. Any major sideways tension on the cover will pressure the hinge, eventually popping it off.

Completed!

Easy Projects for Smaller Kids

Spending time doing something constructive and imaginative for your children is indeed a rewarding activity for parents. Nowadays, parents are searching for enjoyable and interesting DIY projects for children with summer breaks in progress that can have them

productively busy during the scorching, sparkling summers! We share some easy ideas for woodworking projects that will no doubt help your child learn new skills, stimulate children's imagination, as well as keep them entertained during holidays. Read on to pick up some cool wooden crafts for children!

Devoting time doing something productive and imaginative for your children is indeed a rewarding activity for parents. These are some basic wood related projects for kids that stimulate children's imagination and provide you some pleasant and cheerful instants with them!

Feeder for Birds

Building bird feeders is a process that needs just a few supplies!

Tools and materials

- A log or A branch of wood (about 5" wide and 16" long)
- Machine to drill
- Pen Marker
- Rope, 9-11 centimeters long
- Feed for birds
- A butter knife

Easy Steps

1. Keeping the wood in its rough condition., make unplanned lengthwise markings for drilling holes on the branch.

2. Using the drill machine, drill about 10 to 14 holes into the log of measuring 1" by 1".

3. Drill two holes on the top part of the log then hang the feeder by the rope.

4. Ask your child to combine peanut butter with bird feed.

5. Fill in the spaces with a mixture of bird feed and peanut butter with a butter knife.

6. Hang out the feeder to attract feathery pals!

Flatboats

A remarkably easy woodwork activity for kindergarteners. Include your little ones in this project to create a lovely flatboat!

Tools and materials

- A machine for drilling
- A saw
- A thick branch
- 6-inch-long stick
- A Colorful Cloth
- Glue
- Scissors

Easy Steps

1. Using a saw, cut flat round discs of 2 inches from the thick branch.
2. Drill out a hole large enough to attach the stick upright into the discs.
3. Cut the fabric into a triangular form and attach the cloth's broadside to the stick using glue.
4. Also, use adhesive on the flat disc to secure the flagstick.

There's a flatboat able to swim!

3. Sign Address

The creation of an address sign for the house is another fun carpentry activity for kids!

Tools and materials

- A Branch (4 inches by 10 inches)
- A regular wooden board (8 inches by 14 inches)
- Nails
- Sand paper
- Hammer
- Paint (any cheerful color)
- Polishing or varnishing the wood
- Paintbrush Paints

Easy Steps

1. To get rid of the roughness, take a sandpaper and rub it to smooth the wooden surface.

2. With paint and paintbrush, write your address on the plain wooden board. Alternatively, for neatness, use pre-made stencils. Leave the paint to dry.

3. Protect the paint by applying polish.

4. Using nails, attach the branch to the board.

5. Make a hole in the front porch and fix the sign in it.

Done! The address sign is ready!

5. Coasters of wood

Include all your kids in creating these stylish and simple wooden coasters, a fascinating woodworking project for children!

Tools and materials

- A heavy branch (5 to 4 inches in width)
- Sand Paper
- A saw
- Paintbrush
- Paints in acrylic

Easy Steps

1. Using the saw, remove small round discs from the thick branch, half an inch thick. To create a set, size out 6 round discs.

2. Using sandpaper, scrape all sides of every disc to smoothen.

3. To make designs, apply acrylic paints, or just color them in single colors. Leave the color to dry.

To safeguard the paint, cover the coasters in varnish. Before using them, allow to dry!

5. Holder of Pencil

This one is the easiest wood projects to do with your kids in the kindergarten!

Tools and materials

- A saw

- A board of wood (12" by 12")
- A very good adhesive
- Paintbrushes
- Paint
- Sandpaper

Easy Steps

1. Cut out the wooden sheet into 4 planks of the same dimension (4" by 3") and 1 plank (3" by 3") to be used as the frame, using a saw.

2. To smooth off the coarse corners, use sandpaper.

3. Use a good glue to stick all four boards of the same size to create a rectangle box without cover.

4. Fix the rectangular frame onto the narrower board as the foundation.

5. Once the glue dries, help your child paint the pencil holder. When the paint dries off, use it as a pencil holder!

Wood paperweight

Often simple wood projects, just as this one, are pleasant and exhilarating too! Here we are going to build a paperweight from a block of wood.

Tools and materials

- A cube of wood (4 inches by 4 inches)
- Paint in black
- Paints in bright acrylic (2 to 3 shades)
- Paintbrush
- Paints

Easy Steps

1. With bright contrasting shades, paint all parts of the block of wood. Leave it to dry.

2. Make dots on either side with black paint. Take idea from some play dice you must have.

Until using this masterpiece for paperweight, let the paint dry!

Box of wood

A great place to store knick-knacks for your kiddo or keep those knick-knacks away!

Tools and materials

- 2 wooden board (3" by 3")
- 4 wooden board (3" by 5")
- 1 circular wooden bead
- Golden Color Paints
- Strong adhesive
- Any ornamental stones

Easy Steps

1. Taking one long board as the foundation, use the adhesive to stick two short and two long boards horizontally on it to make a rectangular box.
2. Using the last board, make it the box's cover. Fix the wood bead as a handle in the middle.
3. Before coloring the box with the gold ink, let the adhesive dry up completely.
4. Fix decorative objects randomly to make to box more charming.

Cap Rack

A creative idea for your child's space to make an awesome home décor concept!

Tools and materials

- A rectangle wooden board (9 inches by 3 inches)
- Nails
- 7 or 8 hooks of metal
- Hammer
- Black Paint
- White Paint (or of your choice)

Easy Steps

1. Take the wooden panel and randomly put the metal hooks and attach on.
2. To paint the plank, first spray white paint for base paint. Allow drying the paint.
3. Then randomly apply black spray paint to provide a darkened effect at different locations.
4. When the color has dried off, hang the rack in the space of your kiddo!

Bookends

You might carry out this design for a project if you were searching for solutions to hold your child's books in proper order. The best way for children to be carefully arranged for their books.

Tools and materials

- Two heavy wood circles (6-7 inches in diameter)
- Saw
- Varnish
- Sandpaper

Easy Steps

1. Take a roundel and slice off one side to make a flat end.

2. To chafe the rough edges of the wood, use sandpaper.

3. Let them shine naturally and with luster by varnishing the wooden roundel. Allow them to dry. Just let them dry properly. You also may paint or use the bookend in its normal state if you like!

Porcupine Craft

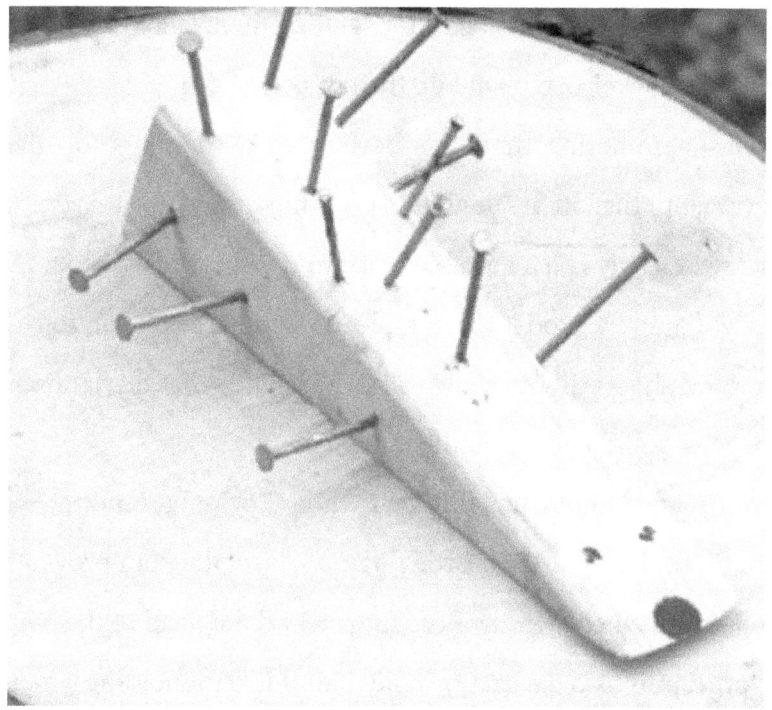

Crafts involving wood, hammers, and nails have always been a hit. Cute woodworking exercise for the children! Using the hammer and nails to create this beautiful wooden porcupine is a pleasurable time for kids. This is a simple craft for preschoolers and big kids, too.

Easy Steps

We begin this project by taking a small piece of 2×4 and cutting it from corner to corner to create two triangular forms. Then, we sand, we sand, and we sand until they are soft and smooth.

Sanding is an essential aspect of a woodworking project since certain aspects in life actually require time to get them right.

We painted on the eyes and nose after sanding them smoothly. Also, a permanent marker pen would do the trick.

Finally, it's hammering time! It's best to go outdoors to do the hammering, but the kitchen table can be as nice as any for this craft. Outdoors will always be a suitable place to do this craft, of course. If you've got a really good kitchen table, don't do the craft on top of it! A plywood sheet will fit really well to guarantee that no hammer or nail traces would end up on the table.

Kids enjoy using clothespins or pliers while they're hammering. It is a brilliant trick to spare the little fingers. The clothespin provides bit more distance between the little fingers and the head of the nail. Many clothespins also have a tiny hole that's ideal for holding a nail. Kids find nails with a little bigger head simpler to pound. Although if you choose nails with small heads, they may appear more like porcupine quill, these little porcupines are more than just beautiful.

Catapult

Do you really want to learn how to construct a catapult? Yes? Me, too. It's really very quick to make this homemade catapult, and it's a great activity for children of all ages!

Tools and materials

- 6 wooden dowels (ours are 3 ft. long) you can get them at
- Walmart, the hobby shop, or the hardware store.
- 9 large bands of rubber
- A small cup of plastic or paper
- Single punch hole
- Scissors
- Small balls, paper balls, pom poms, or

Easy Steps

Let's start with constructing the structure of the catapult, or the catapult's base. Using three wooden dowels, turn them into a triangle by strapping the corners with large rubber bands.

Then you attach the next three dowels like a triangle as well, but they should be standing up like a pyramid or a tepee. Attach one at a time from any corner of the first triangle, heading upward. Then tie them on top with a rubber band in the middle.

Second, take your cup of plastic and punch three holes in it, placed equally across the top of the cup.

Break three bands of rubber in half and tie them into the cup through the gaps.

It is necessary to attach the other ends of the rubber bands to the top portion of the catapult and two corners at the bottom. To make this work, you may need some larger rubber bands. If the rubber bands are not big enough, attach to the ends of three more runner bands so that they may extend down the dowels all the way.

Creating a homemade catapult

The Catapult Fire!

Place the ball in the cup, pull it back and let it go!!! You have completed the construction of a catapult. People will be impressed. (And there's no need to remind them how easy it was!)

These are simple woodworking exercises you should try with your children. You can also oversee the children in carrying out these tasks because they may find them a little boring in using a hammer, nail, saw, and other tools! These activities are full of great learning.

What Kids are learning by hammering:

Strengthening finger muscles and writing hands

Hand-Eye Co-ordination

Developing fine motor capabilities while handling nails

Concentration and patience

Help Your Children's Wood Creations Last Longer

Try these few things to make the imaginative art of your kid's wood last long.

Sand it all beforehand. It is a sensory sensation, as well. Tell your child to get a rough piece of wood, now help them smooth it and inquire if they want more rough or smooth.

Keep a careful watch on the bit of adhesive. To stick well, go two parts at a time, lock the fused pieces with the clamps, and let them dry thoroughly.

Ask your child to add color to their designs using their choice markers or drawings after confirming that glue is set up.

Conclusion

For children and their parents, woodworking can be a fantastic bonding activity, and even families with little or no experience can teach it to their children.

Start quick, be secure, and choose a project that is exciting and useful.

And even if you are uncertain of yourself, give woodworking a shot. Your children might enjoy it, and for generations to come, you will teach them a talent that can support you all.

Industrial crafts, including woodwork, provide long-term Advantages for youngsters. Some of these advantages are:

Personal Growth: Construction is a perfect opportunity for children to strengthen their visual abilities and coordination. It is also a perfect means of improving talents, patience, and faith in problem-solving.

Creativity: Kids' wood building kits are an excellent opportunity for kids to release their imaginative minds to develop fresh designs with the materials supplied. Woodworking demands a lot of consistency and analytical logic, too.

It increases the child's thinking capacity and can even play a major role in several other aspects of the child's existence.

Bonding Activity: Woodworking activities for children are a perfect opportunity to connect if you include it as an enjoyable activity and at the same moment improve the potential of your child to create. You may even opt to jointly try the project and develop closeness with your children.

www.ingramcontent.com/pod-product-compliance
Lightning Source LLC
Chambersburg PA
CBHW071500080526
44587CB00014B/2161